Gourmet's weekends

Gourmet's

weekends

From the Editors of Gourmet

Food Photographs by Romulo A. Yanes

Condé Nast Books   Random House

New York

Copyright © 1995
The Condé Nast Publications Inc.
All rights reserved under International
and Pan-American Copyright
Conventions. Published in the
United States by Random House, Inc.,
New York, and simultaneously in
Canada by Random House of Canada
Limited, Toronto.

LIBRARY OF CONGRESS
CATALOGING-IN-PUBLICATION DATA

Gourmet's Weekends / from the editors
of Gourmet. – 1st ed.
　　　p. cm
　Includes index.
　ISBN 0-679-44568-4: $25.00
　1. Cookery. 2. Entertaining.
　3. Menus. I. Gourmet
TX714.G683　1995
642.4 – DC20　95-9679
　　　　　　　CIP

Some of the recipes in this work
were published previously in
Gourmet Magazine.

Manufactured in the United States
of America on acid-free paper

98765432 24689753 23456789
First Edition

🕐　indicates that a recipe can be
　　made in 45 minutes or less.

🕐+ indicates that a recipe can be
　　made in 45 minutes or less, but
　　requires additional unattended
　　time.

All informative text in this book
was written by Diane Keitt and
Judith Tropea.

Jacket recipes: "Chilled Tomato
Basil Soup" and "Garlic Baguette
Toasts" (page 121).

For Condé Nast Books

Jill Cohen, *President*

Ellen Maria Bruzelius,
　Direct Marketing Director
Pat Van Note,
　Product Development Manager
Lucille Friedman,
　Fulfillment Manager
Tina Kessler,
　Direct Marketing Administrator
Jennifer Metz,
　Direct Marketing Associate
Diane Pesce,
　Prepress Services Manager
Serafino J. Cambareri,
　Quality Control Manager

For *Gourmet* Books

Diane Keitt, *Director*
Judith Tropea, *Editor*

For *Gourmet* Magazine

Gail Zweigenthal, *Editor-in-Chief*

Zanne Early Zakroff,
　Executive Food Editor
Kemp Miles Minifie,
　Senior Food Editor
Alexis M. Touchet,
　Associate Food Editor
Amy Mastrangelo, *Food Editor*
Elizabeth Vought, *Food Editor*
Lori Walther, *Food Editor*
Peggy Anderson, *Assistant Food Editor*

Romulo A. Yanes, *Photographer*
Marjorie H. Webb, *Stylist*
Nancy Purdum, *Stylist*

Produced in association with
Media Projects Incorporated

Carter Smith, *Executive Editor*
Anne Wright, *Project Editor*
John W. Kern, *Production Editor*
Marilyn Flaig, *Indexer*

Salsgiver Coveney Associates Inc.,
　Jacket and Book Design
Laura Howell, *Illustrator*

The text of this book was set in New Baskerville
and Franklin Gothic by Salsgiver Coveney
Associates Inc. The four-color separations were
done by The Color Company, Seiple Lithographers,
and Applied Graphic Technologies. The book
was printed and bound at R. R. Donnelley and Sons.
The paper is Citation Web Gloss, Westvāco.

Acknowledgments

The editors of Gourmet Books would like to thank all colleagues and freelancers who contributed to *Gourmet's Weekends*. Foremost, we would like to thank Zanne Early Zakroff and Leslie Glover Pendleton for a book that is both inventive and practical, and Alexis M. Touchet, Lori Walther, Liz Vought, and Peggy Anderson, for testing an amazing amount of recipes in a very short time. Special thanks also goes to Kemp Minifie who graciously answered our many culinary questions and to Hobby McKenney, Elaine Richard, Anne Wright, John Kern, Toni Rachiele, and Caragh Rockwood for their editorial assistance.

Throughout the book you will find exquisite food photographs by Romulo A. Yanes, styled by Marjorie Webb and Nancy Purdum, as well as extraordinary photographs of seasonal beauty from Lans Christensen, Lisa Koenig, Angelo Lomeo, Mathias Oppersdorff, Adam Woolfitt, and Romulo A. Yanes.

Gerald Asher, *Gourmet*'s Wine Editor, recommended all the beverages for our menus and we appreciate the care that he took with each selection. Also, we would like to thank Karen Salsgiver and Laura Howell of Salsgiver Coveney Associates Inc. for a winning design that captures the joy of weekends.

Table of Contents

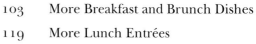

Introduction

For more than 50 years, *Gourmet* has been known as the magazine of good living. And to us, cherished friends, delicious food, and relaxed gatherings are all part of the good life. So, when the idea of putting together a cookbook for weekend entertaining was proposed, I knew immediately that it was ideal for us.

Inviting friends to spend the weekend presents wonderful possibilities, but it takes time to plan special activities *and* fabulous meals. Over the past months, our editors have put themselves in *your* shoes as the host. The result is *Gourmet's Weekends,* a little book that says volumes about casual entertaining at its very best. Now you can organize your next get-together without a lot of fuss.

Our book offers four complete weekends filled with delightful menus: a Spring Garden Weekend, a Summer Beach House Weekend, a Fall Foliage Weekend, and a Winter Ski Weekend. From inviting Friday-evening dinners to unforgettable Sunday-afternoon send-offs, our Executive Food Editor, Zanne Zakroff, has developed a collection of outstanding complementary menus. Each meal perfectly suits the season and activity planned and always takes advantage of seasonal goodness.

But that's not all. To give you myriad options for mixing and matching dishes, we've added over 100 additional recipes in organized chapters: More Breakfast and Brunch Dishes, More Lunch Entrées, More Dinner Entrées, More Side Dishes, More Desserts, and More Snacks and Beverages. If you'd like to substitute a recipe in one of the menus, simply turn to the appropriate chapter. Or, if you're looking for a midnight snack or an afternoon cocktail, flip to the chapter on snacks and beverages.

Because we know that it is difficult to cook exceptional meals and still have time to spend with your guests, this book is filled with shortcuts. You'll find many quick recipes that can be prepared in 45 minutes or less (these are indicated in the text and index with a ☽ symbol, or a ☽+ symbol when additional unattended time is required). And, to help you plan ahead, dishes that can be made in advance are listed on the first page of each menu. Also, you will notice that some menus include store-bought items (bread) or simple dishes that can be made without a recipe (green salads and sliced-fruit desserts). Beverage selections are also suggested. With one quick call to your wine merchant, you can order a delivery and have one less thing to think about.

With a bit of imagination *Gourmet's Weekends* can accommodate the needs of any cook. Transform our beach house weekend into a getaway to the mountains, or simply use one of the menus from our ski weekend to treat your neighbors to a winter warm-up by the fire. Or peruse our recipe chapters to put together a menu of your own. We'd be delighted!

Time with friends should be special, and now it can be, with *Gourmet's Weekends.*

Gail Zweigenthal
Editor-in-Chief

Jumbleberry Pie and Peach and Brown Sugar Ice Cream (page 184)

spring

garden
weekend

Suddenly *everything* is green and bursting with color. Spring has

sprung, and your local farmers market is brimming with tender

lettuces, tart young rhubarb stalks, baby scallions, aromatic herbs,

and much, much more. Come celebrate the flavors of the season

with a collection of very special menus filled with goodness from the

garden. And don't forget to snip a few tulips for the table.

This light yet satisfying spring menu offers a relaxed welcome for weekend guests. Three of the recipes can be prepared ahead, and the other two are quick and easy. The Mussel and Parsley Soup, made with the freshest mollusks, is a delicious, velvety smooth dish. It is paired with a moist Cheddar bread and an easy salad. But the *pièce de résistance* is our warm Baked Rhubarb with Apricot. To use fresh rhubarb, discard the leaves and simply wash the stalks, do not peel them. When fresh rhubarb is out of season, substitute a 1 1/4-pound package of frozen rhubarb and add 15 minutes to the cooking time.

Make-Ahead Information

• Cheddar Herb Bread may be made 5 days ahead and chilled, or up to 2 weeks ahead and frozen, wrapped tightly in foil.

• Orange Thins with Anise: Dough may be made 3 months ahead and frozen, wrapped well. Cookies may be made 5 days ahead and kept in an airtight container.

• Mussel and Parsley Soup may be prepared, in part, 1 day ahead and kept chilled, covered. You will need about 15 minutes to finalize.

A Casual Friday Dinner

Mussel and Parsley Soup

Cheddar Herb Bread

Arugula, Boston Lettuce, and Radish Salad

Baked Rhubarb with Apricot

Orange Thins with Anise

Columbia Crest Chardonnay 1993

Serves 6

Mussel and Parsley Soup

7	pounds mussels
1 1/2	cups dry white wine
1 1/2	cups onion, chopped fine
1/2	stick (1/4 cup) unsalted butter
4	large egg yolks
3/4	cup milk
1/2	cup fresh parsley leaves, chopped fine
	freshly ground black pepper to taste
3	tablespoons fresh lemon juice, or to taste

Scrub mussels well in several changes of water and scrape off beards. Rinse mussels. In a large kettle combine mussels and wine and bring to a boil over high heat. Steam mussels, covered, shaking kettle occasionally, 4 to 6 minutes, or until shells have opened, and discard any unopened shells. Drain mussels in a colander set over a bowl, reserving liquid, and strain reserved liquid through a fine sieve lined with several layers of rinsed and squeezed cheesecloth into a large measuring cup. Add enough water to liquid to measure 6 cups total and reserve mussel liquid mixture. Remove mussels from shells, discarding all but 12 shells, and pull off mantles (tough black rims) from sides of mussels.

In a large saucepan cook onion in butter over moderately low heat, stirring, until softened. Add reserved mussel liquid mixture and bring to a boil. Simmer mussel broth 20 minutes. *Mussels and broth may be made 1 day ahead and cooled, uncovered, before chilling, covered.*

In a bowl whisk together yolks and milk and add about 1 cup mussel broth in a stream, whisking. Transfer mixture to pan, whisking, and add parsley, pepper, and lemon juice. Cook soup over low heat, stirring, 10 minutes, but do not let boil, and stir in mussels.

Divide soup among 6 bowls and garnish each serving with 2 shells. Makes about 10 cups, serving 6.

Photo on page 12

Cheddar Herb Bread

2 1/2	cups all-purpose flour
1 1/2	teaspoons salt
1/2	teaspoon baking soda
2	teaspoons baking powder
1/8	teaspoon cayenne
1	teaspoon dried thyme, crumbled
1	teaspoon dried rosemary, crumbled
1	teaspoon coarsely ground black pepper
1 1/2	cups coarsely grated sharp Cheddar cheese
3/4	cup minced fresh flat-leafed parsley leaves
2	tablespoons vegetable shortening, melted and cooled
2	tablespoons sugar
2	large eggs, beaten lightly
1	cup buttermilk

Preheat oven to 350° F. and butter and flour a loaf pan, 9¼- by 5¼- by 2¾-inches.

In a bowl combine well with a fork flour, salt, baking soda, baking powder, cayenne, thyme, rosemary, pepper, Cheddar, and parsley. In a large bowl stir together shortening and sugar. Add eggs and combine well. Stir in buttermilk, combining well, and add flour mixture, stirring until just combined.

Transfer batter to prepared pan and bake in middle of oven 45 to 55 minutes, or until a tester comes out clean. Cool bread in pan on a rack 15 minutes. Loosen edges with a knife and turn bread right side up on rack. Cool bread 2 hours. *Bread may be made 5 days ahead and chilled or 2 weeks ahead and frozen, wrapped tightly in foil.*

Arugula, Boston Lettuce, and Radish Salad

2 large bunches *arugula*, coarse stems discarded and leaves washed thoroughly and spun dry (about 8 cups packed)

1 small head Boston lettuce, separated into leaves

1 cup sliced radish (about 6 large radishes)

3 tablespoons olive oil

1 tablespoon fresh lemon juice

In a large bowl combine *arugula*, Boston lettuce, and radish. Drizzle oil over salad and toss gently. Sprinkle salad with lemon juice and salt and pepper to taste and toss. Serves 6.

Baked Rhubarb with Apricot

1 cup apricot nectar

1/2 cup firmly packed light brown sugar

1/4 cup very hot water

3 tablespoons unsalted butter, cut into bits

1/2 teaspoon vanilla

1/8 teaspoon almond extract

1 1/2 pounds rhubarb, trimmed and cut into 1/2-inch pieces (about 6 cups)

Accompaniment: vanilla ice cream or whipped cream

Preheat oven to 350° F.

In an 11- by 7-inch baking dish combine well all ingredients. Bake dessert in middle of oven, stirring very gently halfway through baking, 30 minutes, or until rhubarb is soft, and cool 10 minutes.

Serve dessert with ice cream or whipped cream. Serves 6.

Orange Thins with Anise

1/2 cup vegetable shortening at room temperature

2 tablespoons unsalted butter, softened

1 cup sugar

1/2 teaspoon vanilla

3/4 teaspoon anise seeds, crushed lightly

1 1/2 tablespoons freshly grated orange zest

1/4 cup fresh orange juice (from about 1/2 orange)

1 1/2 cups all-purpose flour

1 1/2 teaspoons baking powder

1/2 teaspoon baking soda

1/4 teaspoon salt

confectioners' sugar for dusting cookies

Preheat oven to 350° F.

In a bowl with an electric mixer beat together shortening, butter, and sugar. Add vanilla, anise seeds, zest, and orange juice, beating until smooth. Into bowl sift together flour, baking powder, baking soda, and salt and blend dough well. Chill dough 15 minutes, or until slightly firm. On a sheet of wax paper form dough into a log 1½ inches in diameter, using paper as a guide. Freeze dough, wrapped in wax paper and foil, 1 hour, or until firm. *Dough may be made 3 months ahead and frozen, wrapped well.*

Cut dough log into ⅛-inch slices with a sharp knife and bake 2 inches apart on ungreased baking sheets in middle of oven 8 to 10 minutes, or until edges are just golden. Transfer cookies immediately with a metal spatula to racks and cool. Sift confectioners' sugar lightly over cookies. *Cookies may be made 5 days ahead and kept in an airtight container.* Makes about 50 cookies.

After a rushed week, there is nothing quite as pampering as our leisurely breakfast. Be sure to bake the coffeecake the day before so that you, too, can enjoy a Saturday-morning sleep in. This cake, made with sour cream, will stay moist, and you will need only minutes to prepare the espresso glaze. The ham steak also requires a simple glaze before it is quickly broiled. You can serve the *frittata* either warm or at room temperature with equal success. For a warm *frittata*, sauté the vegetables and herbs, then wait until your guests amble into the kitchen before adding the eggs.

Make-Ahead Information

- The cake for the Coffee Coffeecake with Espresso Glaze may be made 1 day ahead and kept wrapped well at room temperature. You will need an additional 15 minutes for the glaze.

Lazy Morning Wake-Up

Coffee Coffeecake with Espresso Glaze

Red Onion, Scallion, and Tarragon Frittata

Honey-Mustard-Glazed Ham Steak

Juice

Coffee

Serves 6

Coffee Coffeecake with Espresso Glaze

For cake

- 2 cups sifted all-purpose flour
- 1 teaspoon baking powder
- 1/2 teaspoon baking soda
- 1/4 teaspoon salt
- 1 1/2 sticks (3/4 cup) unsalted butter, softened
- 1 cup sugar
- 2 large eggs
- 2 teaspoons vanilla
- 1 cup sour cream
- 2 tablespoons instant espresso powder dissolved in 1 tablespoon hot water

For glaze

- 2 to 3 tablespoons strong brewed coffee
- 1 1/2 teaspoons instant espresso powder
- 3/4 cup confectioners' sugar, sifted

Make cake:

Preheat oven to 350° F. and generously butter an 8-inch (1½-quart) bundt pan.

Into a bowl sift together flour, baking powder, baking soda, and salt. In another bowl with an electric mixer cream butter. Add sugar gradually, beating, and beat until light and fluffy. Add eggs, 1 at a time, beating well after each addition, and beat in vanilla. Add flour mixture alternately with sour cream, beginning and ending with flour mixture and blending batter after each addition. Transfer about one third of batter to a small bowl and stir in espresso mixture until combined well. Spoon half of plain batter into prepared pan, spreading evenly, and spoon coffee batter over it, spreading evenly. Spoon remaining plain batter on top, spreading evenly. Bake cake in middle of oven 55 to 60 minutes, or until golden and a tester comes out clean. Cool cake 30 minutes in pan on a rack and invert onto rack. Cool cake completely. *Cake may be prepared up to this point 1 day ahead and kept wrapped well at room temperature.*

Make glaze:

In a bowl stir together 2 tablespoons brewed coffee and espresso powder until powder is dissolved and add confectioners' sugar. Stir glaze until combined well. If necessary add more of remaining 1 tablespoon coffee to reach a pourable consistency.

Pour glaze over cake and let stand 10 minutes, or until glaze is set.

Photo on page 16

Red Onion, Scallion, and Tarragon Frittata

- 1 large red onion, halved lengthwise and sliced thin lengthwise
- 1 cup chopped scallion (white and green parts)
- 2 tablespoons olive oil
- 1 tablespoon minced fresh tarragon leaves or 1/2 teaspoon dried, crumbled
- 1 large garlic clove, minced and mashed to a paste with 1/4 teaspoon salt
- 6 large eggs, beaten lightly

Preheat oven to 400° F.

In a non-stick ovenproof skillet (cover handle with foil) measuring 8 to 8½- inches across the bottom cook onion and scallion in oil over moderately low heat, stirring, until softened. Stir in tarragon, garlic paste, and salt and pepper to taste and cook until garlic is fragrant, about 30 seconds. Pour eggs into skillet and cook over moderate heat, without stirring, until set on bottom but still runny on top, 3 to 5 minutes. Bake *frittata* in middle of oven until top is set, 4 to 6 minutes.

Serve *frittata*, cut into wedges, warm or at room temperature. Serves 6.

Honey-Mustard-Glazed Ham Steak

1/3 cup honey mustard
1/4 teaspoon ground cloves
2 1-pound ham steaks (about 1/2 inch thick), edges scored lightly at 1-inch intervals

Preheat broiler.

In a small saucepan stir together mustard and cloves and heat over moderate heat, stirring occasionally, until warm.

Rinse ham steaks under cold water and pat dry. Arrange steaks on rack of a broiler pan and brush with half of glaze. Broil steaks about 4 inches from heat 3 minutes. Turn steaks and brush with remaining glaze. Broil steaks 3 to 4 minutes more, or until heated through and lightly browned.

Slice each steak on the diagonal into 3 pieces. Serves 6.

To fully enjoy the gorgeous blossoms in your spring garden we offer a colorful alfresco lunch. Begin with a fresh salad of seasonal mixed lettuces: tender Bibb, Lollo rosso (an Italian red-leaf), oak leaf (a bronze-leaf), mâche (or lamb's lettuce), and the somewhat bitter *radicchio.* A slice of Brie and a lively lemon- and orange-flavored dressing make this a delightful starter. Carrot Soup with Croutons, a warming dish with crunch, and our smooth and creamy Cottage Cheese Spinach Tart follow. For dessert, easy and delicious Glazed Strawberries will surely prompt oohs and aahs!

Make-Ahead Information

- The carrot soup may be made 2 days ahead and chilled, covered. The accompanying croutons also may be made 2 days ahead and kept in an airtight container.

- The citrus dressing for the Mixed Lettuces with Citrus Dressing may be made 1 day ahead and chilled, covered.

- The tart shell for the Cottage Cheese Spinach Tart may be made 1 day ahead and kept covered at room temperature.

Lunch in the Garden

Mixed Lettuces with Citrus Dressing

Carrot Soup with Croutons

Cottage Cheese Spinach Tart

Glazed Strawberries

Greenwood Ridge Anderson Valley Merlot 1992

Serves 6

Mixed Lettuces with Citrus Dressing

3	tablespoons fresh lemon juice
1 1/2	tablespoons fresh orange juice
1/2	cup olive oil
1/8	teaspoon Tabasco, or to taste
12	cups mixed lettuces such as mâche, Lollo rosso, Bibb, and oak leaf, torn into pieces
1/2	cup thinly sliced *radicchio*

Garnish: ornamental kale leaves for lining plates
Accompaniment: 6 Brie cheese slices

In a large bowl whisk together juices and salt and pepper to taste. Add oil in a stream, whisking, and whisk until emulsified. Whisk in Tabasco. *Dressing may be made 1 day ahead and chilled, covered.* Add lettuces and *radicchio* and toss well.

Line 6 plates with kale and top with salad. Arrange a Brie slice on each salad. Serves 6.

Photo on page 20

Carrot Soup with Croutons

1 1/2	pounds carrots, sliced
1	large onion, minced
3	tablespoons unsalted butter
1/2	teaspoon dried thyme, crumbled
1/2	teaspoon sugar
6	cups chicken broth
	For croutons
2	tablespoons unsalted butter
2	tablespoons vegetable oil
4	1/2-inch slices homemade-type white bread, crusts removed and cut into 1/2-inch cubes

In a saucepan sweat carrots and onion in butter with thyme, sugar, and salt to taste, covered directly with a buttered round of wax paper and the pan lid, over moderate heat, stirring occasionally, 8 minutes. Add broth and bring to a boil. Simmer mixture, covered, 25 minutes, or until carrots are very soft.

In a food processor or blender purée mixture in batches and transfer to a saucepan. Bring soup to a simmer and thin with water to desired consistency. Season soup with salt and pepper and keep warm. *Soup may be made 2 days ahead and cooled, uncovered, before chilling, covered.*

Make croutons:
In a large skillet heat butter and oil over moderately high heat until hot and sauté bread cubes, tossing, until golden brown. Transfer croutons with a slotted spoon to paper towels to drain. *Croutons may be made 2 days ahead and kept in an airtight container.*

Serve soup topped with croutons. Serves 6.

Cottage Cheese Spinach Tart

         pastry dough for a 9-inch tart
         (recipe follows)
         raw rice for weighting shell
    1/3 cup minced onion
      3 tablespoons unsalted butter
    1/2 cup cooked, well-squeezed,
         and chopped spinach
    1/4 cup milk
         freshly grated nutmeg to taste
      4 large eggs
  1 1/2 cups creamed cottage cheese
    1/2 cup freshly grated Parmesan cheese

Preheat oven to 425° F.

Roll dough out ⅛ inch thick on a floured surface and fit into a 9-inch flan or tart pan with a removable fluted rim. Prick bottom of shell with a fork and chill 30 minutes. Line shell with wax paper and fill with rice. Bake shell on a baking sheet in lower third of oven 15 minutes. Remove rice and paper carefully and bake shell 10 minutes more, or until golden. Cool shell in pan on a rack. *Tart shell may be made 1 day ahead and kept covered at room temperature.*

Reduce temperature to 350° F.

In a skillet cook onion in 2 tablespoons butter over moderate heat, stirring, until softened. Add spinach and cook, stirring, 2 minutes. Remove skillet from heat and stir in milk, nutmeg, and salt and pepper to taste. Cool spinach mixture. In a bowl beat together eggs, cottage cheese, and Parmesan and stir in spinach mixture.

Pour filling into shell and dot with remaining tablespoon butter, cut into bits. Bake tart in oven 35 to 40 minutes, or until a knife inserted in center comes out clean, and cool in pan on a rack 10 minutes. Serves 6.

☺+ Pastry Dough

  1 1/4 cups all-purpose flour
    3/4 stick (6 tablespoons) cold unsalted
         butter, cut into bits
      2 tablespoons cold vegetable shortening
    1/4 teaspoon salt
  2 to 4 tablespoons ice water

In a bowl with a pastry blender or in a food processor blend or pulse together flour, butter, shortening, and salt until mixture resembles meal. Add 2 tablespoons ice water and toss or pulse until water is incorporated. Add enough remaining ice water if necessary to form a dough and form dough into a disk. Lightly dust dough with flour and chill, wrapped in wax paper, 1 hour.

☺+ Glazed Strawberries

      2 12-ounce jars red currant jelly
  1 1/2 pounds strawberries with stems intact
         (about 1 1/2 pints)
         small fluted paper cups if desired

Line a shallow baking pan with wax paper.

In a saucepan melt jelly over moderate heat, whisking, until smooth. Holding each strawberry by its stem, dip it in red currant jelly, letting excess drip off, and put strawberry on prepared pan. Glaze remaining strawberries in same manner. (If jelly becomes too thick, reheat over low heat, stirring.) Chill strawberries 1 hour, or until glaze is set.

Serve strawberries in fluted paper cups if desired. Makes about 36 glazed strawberries.

Our Saturday dinner, filled with the flavors of spring, is very special indeed. Ideally, all the main dishes should be partially prepared ahead of time, so that you can serve this impressive menu with little last-minute fuss. Both the filling and the sauce for the won ton ravioli starter can be made ahead, leaving only minutes to assemble and cook the ravioli. Also, the lamb steak entrée can be put in its marinade up to 8 hours before it is broiled. For dessert, the sorbet, once frozen in pineapple shells, requires only a quick meringue topping.

Make-Ahead Information

- The sorbet for the Pineapple Sorbet with Meringue may be made 2 days ahead and frozen, covered.

- Goat Cheese Ravioli with Garlic Tomato Sauce: The filling *must* be chilled, covered, at least 1 hour, or until cold, and may be made up to 1 day ahead and chilled, covered. The sauce may be made 2 days ahead and chilled, covered.

- The lamb steak for the Lamb London Broil with Rosemary Sauce *must* be marinated at least 2 hours and up to 8 hours, covered and chilled.

A Taste of Spring Dinner

**Goat Cheese Ravioli
with Garlic Tomato Sauce**

**Lamb London Broil
with Rosemary Sauce**

Rice with Parsley and Toasted Almonds

Watercress Salad Vinaigrette

Pineapple Sorbet with Meringue

Joseph Phelps Napa Valley
Cabernet Sauvignon 1990

for dessert,
Geyser Peak Russian River Valley
Late Harvest Riesling 1993

Serves 6

Goat Cheese Ravioli with Garlic Tomato Sauce

For filling

3/4	pound soft mild goat cheese such as Montrachet, at room temperature
3	tablespoons ricotta cheese
1/3	cup finely chopped prosciutto (about 2 ounces)
1/4	cup finely chopped fresh basil leaves
1/2	teaspoon freshly grated lemon zest
1	large egg, beaten lightly

For sauce

3	large garlic cloves, sliced thin
1/4	cup olive oil
1	28-ounce can plum tomatoes, drained and chopped fine
1 1/2	teaspoons fresh thyme leaves
60	won ton wrappers*, thawed if frozen

Garnish: 6 fresh basil sprigs

*available at Asian markets and many supermarkets

Make filling:

In a bowl stir together well filling ingredients and salt and pepper to taste. *Chill filling, covered, at least 1 hour, or until cold, and up to 24 hours.*

Make sauce:

In a heavy skillet cook garlic in oil over moderately low heat, stirring, until it just begins to turn pale golden and discard with a slotted spoon. Add tomatoes. Bring mixture to a boil and boil over moderately high heat, stirring, 10 minutes, or until thick. Stir in thyme and salt and pepper to taste. *Sauce may be made 2 days ahead and chilled, covered.* Keep sauce warm, covered, while preparing and cooking ravioli.

Prepare won ton ravioli with goat cheese filling (procedure follows).

Bring a kettle of salted water to a gentle boil for ravioli.

Cook ravioli in boiling water in batches 2 minutes, or until they rise to surface and are tender. (Do not let water boil vigorously once ravioli have been added.) Transfer ravioli as cooked with a slotted spoon to a dry kitchen towel or paper towels to drain and keep warm.

Arrange ravioli on plates. Spoon sauce over ravioli and garnish each serving with a basil sprig. Serves 6 generously.

Photo on page 24

To Prepare Won Ton Ravioli

Put 1 won ton wrapper on a lightly floured surface and mound 1 tablespoon filling in center of wrapper. Brush edges with water and put a second wrapper over first, pressing down around filling to force out air. Seal edges well and trim excess dough around filling with a decorative cutter or sharp knife. Make more won ton ravioli in same manner with remaining wrappers and filling, transferring them as formed to a dry kitchen towel, and turn them occasionally to dry slightly.

Lamb London Broil with Rosemary Sauce

1   2-inch-thick lamb leg steak (about 2 1/2 pounds), scored 1/4-inch deep on both sides
1/4   cup dry vermouth
1   tablespoon fresh lemon juice
2   tablespoons vegetable oil
1/3   cup minced onion
1 1/2 tablespoons minced fresh rosemary leaves
3   tablespoons unsalted butter at room temperature

Garnish: small fresh rosemary sprigs (about 1/2 inch)

In a shallow baking dish slightly larger than lamb steak whisk together vermouth, lemon juice, oil, onion, and 1 tablespoon minced rosemary. Add lamb and turn to coat well on both sides. *Marinate lamb, covered and chilled, turning occasionally, at least 2 hours and up to 8 hours.* Let lamb come to room temperature before broiling.

Preheat broiler.

In a small bowl beat together butter and remaining ½ tablespoon minced rosemary.

Remove lamb from marinade, reserving marinade, and season with salt and pepper. Broil lamb on rack of a broiler pan about 4 inches from heat, turning once, 16 to 18 minutes for medium-rare. Transfer lamb to a platter and let stand 10 minutes.

Pour any juices that have accumulated on platter into a small saucepan. Add 2 tablespoons of reserved marinade and bring to a boil. Whisk in butter mixture and heat sauce until hot, but do not let boil.

Holding a knife at a 45° angle slice lamb very thin across the grain and pour sauce over it. Garnish lamb with rosemary sprigs. Serves 6.

Rice with Parsley and Toasted Almonds

1   cup finely chopped onion
1/2   stick (1/4 cup) unsalted butter
1 1/2 cups converted rice
3 1/3 cups chicken broth
1/2   cup minced fresh parsley leaves
1/2   cup sliced blanched almonds, toasted and chopped

In a saucepan cook onion in butter over moderately low heat, stirring occasionally, until softened. Add rice and cook, stirring, 1 minute. Add broth and bring to a boil. Simmer mixture, covered, 15 minutes. Stir in parsley and simmer, covered, 3 to 5 minutes, or until rice is tender and all liquid has been absorbed. Stir in almonds and pepper to taste. Serves 6.

Watercress Salad Vinaigrette

1   teaspoon Dijon mustard
1/2 teaspoon sugar
1/4 cup white-wine vinegar
6   tablespoons extra-virgin olive oil
1 1/2 tablespoons walnut oil*
2   bunches watercress, coarse stems discarded

*available at specialty foods shops
and some supermarkets

In a small bowl whisk together mustard, sugar, vinegar, and oils and whisk in salt and pepper to taste. In another bowl toss watercress with vinaigrette. Serves 6.

Pineapple Sorbet with Meringue

For sorbet
1   3 1/2-pound pineapple
1/4 cup granulated sugar, or to taste
1/4 cup fresh lemon juice, or to taste
For meringue
3   large egg whites
   a pinch cream of tartar
3/4 cup granulated sugar, ground to a powder
   in a food processor or blender

confectioners' sugar to taste

Make sorbet:
Halve pineapple lengthwise. With a small sharp knife cut around inside edge of pineapple halves and remove pulp, leaving ¼-inch-thick shells. Pat shells dry and freeze, covered with plastic wrap. Core pineapple pulp and cut into 1-inch pieces. In a food processor purée pulp until smooth and blend in sugar and lemon juice. Transfer mixture to 2 ice cube trays and freeze. Transfer cubes to food processor and blend until light and fluffy. Pack sorbet into pineapple shells, mounding slightly, and freeze, covered with plastic wrap. *Sorbet may be made 2 days ahead and frozen, covered.*
Make meringue:
In a bowl with an electric mixer beat whites until foamy. Add cream of tartar and a pinch salt and beat until whites hold soft peaks. Beat in granulated sugar, 1 tablespoon at a time, and beat until whites hold stiff peaks.
Preheat broiler.
Transfer meringue to a pastry bag fitted with a small star tip and pipe decoratively over sorbet, covering it completely. Sift confectioners' sugar over meringue. Arrange shells on a baking sheet and broil about 6 inches from heat 30 seconds to 1 minute, or until meringue is browned lightly. Serve desserts immediately. Serves 6 generously.

On the final day of the weekend, you'll want to spend as much time as possible with your guests. Luckily, the chicken salad and desserts all can be made ahead. When shopping for the oranges, lemons, and limes for this menu, be aware that thin-skinned fruit will be heavy in weight and have the most juice. Usually small and medium-sized fruit have thinner skins and are lower in cost, so don't be tempted to buy large ones. As with all citrus, skin color has nothing to do with quality. For the chicken salad, use only fresh tarragon. Look for green leaves free of brown spots and store the herb, wrapped in dampened paper towels and plastic wrap, in the refrigerator.

Make-Ahead Information

- Cappuccino Gelato may be made 3 days ahead and frozen, covered.

- Chocolate Nut Cookies may be made 3 days ahead and kept in airtight containers.

- Chicken salad for the Tarragon Chicken Salad with Celery and Grapes may be made 1 day ahead and chilled, covered.

Brunch Alfresco

Orange and Lime Spritzers

**Tarragon Chicken Salad
with Celery and Grapes**

Cappuccino Gelato

Chocolate Nut Cookies

DeLoach Russian River Valley
Sauvignon Blanc 1993

Serves 6

Orange and Lime Spritzers

1	cup water
1/2	cup sugar
	zest of 2 navel oranges removed with a vegetable peeler and chopped
2 1/2	cups strained fresh orange juice (from about 5 navel oranges)
1/3	cup strained fresh lime juice (from about 3 limes)
1	bottle chilled dry sparkling wine

Garnish: 6 orange slices

In a saucepan stir together water and sugar and bring to a boil, stirring until sugar is dissolved. Add zest and simmer 5 minutes. Strain syrup through a fine sieve into a bowl and chill until cold.

Add juices to syrup and divide among 6 tall glasses. Top off drinks with sparkling wine. Add ice cubes if desired and garnish each drink with an orange slice. Makes 6 drinks.

Tarragon Chicken Salad with Celery and Grapes

3	pounds chicken breasts, poached with skin and bones (procedure follows), skin and bones discarded, and cooled meat cut into bite-size pieces (about 4 cups)
1 1/2	cups seedless green grapes, halved lengthwise
1 1/2	cups sliced celery
3	tablespoons minced fresh tarragon leaves
	For dressing
1/3	cup plain yogurt
1/3	cup mayonnaise
1 1/2	tablespoons fresh lemon juice, or to taste
2	teaspoons sugar, or to taste

soft-leafed lettuce leaves for lining plates

In a large bowl combine chicken, grapes, celery, and 2 tablespoons tarragon.

Make dressing:

In a small bowl whisk together dressing ingredients until smooth.

Add dressing to chicken mixture with salt and pepper to taste and combine well. *Salad may be made 1 day ahead and chilled, covered.*

Just before serving stir in remaining tablespoon tarragon. Line 6 salad plates with lettuce leaves and top with salad. Serve salad at room temperature or chilled. Serves 6.

To Poach Chicken Breasts

whole chicken breasts with skin and bone (about 1 pound each)

In a large saucepan or kettle combine chicken breasts with cold water to cover by 1 inch. Remove chicken and bring water with salt to taste to a boil. Return chicken to pan or kettle and poach at a bare simmer 17 minutes. Remove pan or kettle from heat and cool chicken in liquid 30 minutes. Drain chicken.

Cappuccino Gelato

    5   cups milk
  1/3   cup instant espresso powder
    4   tablespoons cornstarch
1 1/2   cups sugar

In a small bowl whisk ½ cup milk, scalded, into espresso powder, whisking until powder is dissolved. In another small bowl stir ½ cup remaining milk into cornstarch, stirring until cornstarch is dissolved.

In a heavy saucepan combine remaining 4 cups milk and sugar and bring just to a boil, stirring until sugar is dissolved. Stir cornstarch mixture and whisk into milk and sugar mixture. Simmer mixture, whisking, 2 minutes and whisk in espresso mixture. Cool mixture to room temperature and chill, covered, until cold.

Freeze mixture in an ice-cream maker. *Gelato may be made 3 days ahead and frozen, covered.* Makes about 1 quart.

Photo on page 30

Chocolate Nut Cookies

    2   cups all-purpose flour
    1   teaspoon baking powder
  1/4   teaspoon salt
  1/2   cup unsweetened cocoa powder
  1/2   cup walnuts
  2/3   cup plus 2 tablespoons sugar
  2/3   cup almond paste (about 7 ounces)
    1   stick (1/2 cup) unsalted butter, softened
    1   teaspoon vanilla
    2   large egg whites

In a bowl whisk together flour, baking powder, salt, and cocoa powder.

In a food processor grind walnuts fine with 2 tablespoons sugar. Add almond paste and grind until mixture forms a paste.

In another bowl with an electric mixer beat together butter and remaining ⅔ cup sugar. Add nut paste and vanilla and beat until combined well. Beat in flour mixture at low speed until a dough is formed and add whites, beating until incorporated.

Preheat oven to 350° F. and butter 2 baking sheets.

Working with half of dough at a time, roll out dough ¼ inch thick between sheets of plastic wrap. Cut out diamond shapes with a 2-inch-wide cutter and arrange 1½ inches apart on prepared baking sheets. Press ridges into diamonds with tines of a fork and bake in batches in middle of oven 10 minutes. Cool cookies on sheets on a rack 2 minutes and transfer carefully with a spatula to racks to cool completely. *Cookies may be made 3 days ahead and kept in airtight containers.* Makes about 40 cookies.

Photo on page 30

summer

beach house
weekend

Along with clear blue skies and bright sunshine, summer offers plentiful crops of sweet yellow corn, ripe red tomatoes, fragrant herbs, and fresh peaches, plums, and berries. Our delightful weekend takes full advantage of the glorious days, and nights, of the season and all this bounty with six menus – four of them alfresco. Enjoy a relaxing sunset dinner, a fun picnic on the beach, a carefree evening cookout, a leisurely lunch on the deck, and more! ☀

After a drive to the shore on Friday night, your guests will be ready for a good meal. Welcome them with refreshing Rum and Pineapple Fizzes and flavorful Herbed Ricotta with English Muffin Toasts. When it's time for dinner, the broiled tuna, yogurt biscuits, and Sautéed Corn and Red Peppers can be quickly prepared. Purchase only the freshest tuna: its color should be reddish brown and the flesh translucent and firm. No-fuss sliced mango sprinkled with lime juice makes a light, luscious dessert. Choose firm-skinned mangoes that have a fragrant aroma at the stem end. To ripen, keep them at room temperature until tender.

Make-Ahead Information

- Herbed Ricotta with English Muffin Toasts: Toasts may be made 2 days ahead and kept in an airtight container. Ricotta *must* be drained the night before in a fine sieve set over a bowl, chilled and covered. Herbed ricotta spread may be prepared, in part, 4 hours ahead.

A Sunset Dinner

Rum and Pineapple Fizzes

Herbed Ricotta with English Muffin Toasts

Broiled Tuna Steaks with Lemon Black Olive Paste

Chive Yogurt Drop Biscuits

Sautéed Corn and Red Peppers

Mixed Green Salad

Sliced Mango with Lime

Rex Hill Kings Ridge
Oregon Pinot Noir 1992

Serves 6

☼ Rum and Pineapple Fizzes

9 ounces light rum (6 jiggers)
3 cups chilled unsweetened pineapple juice
1/4 cup fresh lime juice
   chilled club soda or seltzer

Garnish: lime slices

In a large pitcher combine rum and juices.

Fill 6 tall glasses with ice cubes and divide rum mixture among them. Top off drinks with club soda or seltzer and garnish with lime slices. Makes 6 drinks.

Photo on page 36

Herbed Ricotta with English Muffin Toasts

4 English muffins, unsplit, cut crosswise into 1/4-inch-wide strips
1/2 stick (1/4 cup) unsalted butter, melted
1 15-ounce container (1 2/3 cups) whole-milk ricotta cheese, drained in a fine sieve set over a bowl, chilled and covered, overnight
1/3 cup thinly sliced scallion greens
1/3 cup minced fresh parsley leaves
3/4 cup minced radish
1/2 teaspoon minced garlic
1/4 cup fresh lemon juice

Garnish: a fresh parsley sprig and sliced radish

Preheat oven to 375° F.

Brush 1 of cut sides of each muffin strip with butter and bake strips in one layer on a baking sheet in middle of oven until golden, 15 to 17 minutes. Cool toasts on a rack. *Toasts keep 2 days in an airtight container at room temperature.*

In a bowl stir together ricotta, scallion, minced parsley, minced radish, garlic, and salt and pepper to taste until combined well. *Spread may be prepared up to this point 4 hours ahead and chilled, covered.* Stir in lemon juice.

Garnish spread with parsley sprig and sliced radish and serve with toasts. Serves 6 as an hors d'oeuvre.

Photo on page 36

Broiled Tuna Steaks with Lemon Black Olive Paste

For topping

1 cup *olivada, tapenade,* or other black olive paste*
2 teaspoons freshly grated lemon zest
2 teaspoons fresh lemon juice
2 garlic cloves, minced
1/3 teaspoon dried thyme, crumbled

6 1-inch-thick tuna steaks (about 2 1/2 pounds total), rinsed, patted dry, and cut into serving pieces
2 tablespoons olive oil
2 tablespoons fine fresh bread crumbs

Accompaniment: lemon wedges

*available at specialty foods shops and some supermarkets

Make topping:

In a small bowl stir together topping ingredients and pepper to taste.

Preheat broiler.

Rub tuna with 1 tablespoon oil and season with pepper. Broil tuna on rack of a broiler pan about 4 inches from heat 6 minutes on each side, or until just cooked through. Spread topping on tuna and sprinkle with bread crumbs. Drizzle bread crumbs with remaining tablespoon oil. Broil tuna 2 to 4 minutes, or until cooked through and crumbs are golden brown.

Serve tuna with lemon wedges. Serves 6.

Chive Yogurt Drop Biscuits

1 3/4 cups all-purpose flour
2 teaspoons baking powder
1/2 teaspoon baking soda
3/4 teaspoon salt
1/2 teaspoon sugar
6 tablespoons finely chopped fresh chives
4 tablespoons cold vegetable shortening
2/3 cup plain yogurt
1/4 cup milk

Preheat oven to 425° F. and butter a baking sheet.

Into a bowl sift together flour, baking powder, baking soda, salt, and sugar. Add chives and shortening and blend until mixture resembles meal. Stir in yogurt and milk and stir until mixture just forms a soft, sticky dough. Drop dough by rounded tablespoons 2 inches apart onto prepared baking sheet and bake in middle of oven 12 to 14 minutes, or until pale golden. Makes about 16 biscuits.

Sautéed Corn and Red Peppers

1 large onion, chopped (about 1 1/2 cups)
2 large red bell peppers, chopped (about 2 1/4 cups)
3 tablespoons olive oil
4 cups corn (cut from about 7 ears)
1/2 cup minced fresh parsley leaves

In a large skillet cook onion and peppers in oil over moderate heat, stirring occasionally, until softened. Add corn and salt and pepper to taste and cook, stirring, until corn is crisp-tender, about 3 minutes. Stir in parsley. Serves 6.

Since everyone is busy gathering chairs, umbrellas, and towels for today's beach outing, and you are putting together the afternoon picnic, it's best to keep breakfast simple, quick, and self-serve. Our menu is easy *and* delicious. Both the Raspberry Corn Muffins, made extra moist with a touch of yogurt, and the crunchy Cashew and Golden Raisin Granola, sweetened with honey, can be made ahead. With the muffins and granola out of the way, simply put on the coffee, pour the juice, and slice some melon.

Make-Ahead Information

- Cashew and Golden Raisin Granola keeps 1 week in an airtight container at room temperature or 2 weeks chilled.

- Raspberry Corn Muffins may be made 1 day ahead and kept in an airtight container.

Serve-Yourself Breakfast

Raspberry Corn Muffins

Cashew and Golden Raisin Granola

Cantaloupe/Honeydew Melon

Coffee
Tea
Juice

Serves 6

Raspberry Corn Muffins

- 1 cup yellow cornmeal
- 1 cup all-purpose flour
- 1/2 cup sugar
- 1 teaspoon baking powder
- 1 teaspoon baking soda
- 1/4 teaspoon salt
- 2 large eggs
- 1 1/4 cups plain yogurt
- 1/2 stick (1/4 cup) unsalted butter, melted and cooled
- 1 cup fresh raspberries

Preheat oven to 375° F. and butter generously twelve ½-cup muffin tins.

In a bowl whisk together cornmeal, flour, sugar, baking powder, baking soda, and salt. In another bowl whisk together eggs, yogurt, and butter. Add flour mixture and stir until just combined. Fold in raspberries gently and divide batter among prepared muffin tins.

Bake muffins in middle of oven 20 minutes, or until a tester comes out clean. Cool muffins in tins on a rack 3 minutes and turn out onto rack to cool completely. *Muffins may be made 1 day ahead and kept in an airtight container.* Makes 12 muffins.

Photo on page 40

Cashew and Golden Raisin Granola

- 3 cups old-fashioned rolled oats
- 1 cup wheat germ
- 1 cup dried unsweetened grated coconut*
- 1 1/2 cups raw cashews, toasted lightly or roasted cashews, chopped coarse
- 1/3 cup honey
- 1/3 cup vegetable oil
- 1/4 cup fresh orange juice
- 3/4 teaspoon salt
- 3/4 teaspoon cinnamon
- 2/3 cup golden raisins

*available at natural foods stores

Preheat oven to 325° F. and lightly oil a roasting pan.

In a large bowl combine oats, wheat germ, coconut, and cashews and toss until combined well. In a small heavy saucepan heat honey, oil, orange juice, salt, and cinnamon over moderate heat, stirring occasionally, until hot but not boiling and pour over oat mixture. Toss granola well. Spread granola in prepared pan and bake in oven, stirring every 5 minutes, until golden, about 30 minutes. Cool granola completely and add raisins. Toss granola lightly. *Granola keeps 1 week in an airtight container at room temperature or 2 weeks chilled.* Makes about 6½ cups.

By late morning everyone will want
to pack up and head for the water.
Our picnic was devised with toting
in mind — marinated olives; sliced,
crisp crudités; ravigote mayonnaise;
and sturdy fudge brownies — all travel
nicely in airtight plastic containers.
The hearty provençale sandwiches, a
traditional picnic favorite in southern
France, are filled with tuna, anchovies,
basil, and tomatoes, and transport well,
wrapped in plastic. To make the sandwiches even easier to handle, leave the
loaves whole and bring along a cutting
board and a good knife to cut them into
wedges at the beach.

Make-Ahead Information

- Olives *must* be marinated for 3 days.
  They keep indefinitely, chilled and covered.

- Butter-Rich Fudge Brownies may be made
  3 days ahead and kept at room temperature,
  covered.

- Ravigote mayonnaise may be made 2 days
  ahead and chilled, covered.

- Provençale Sandwiches with Tuna, Basil,
  and Tomato *must* be weighted and chilled,
  covered, 1 hour. They may be made 4 hours
  ahead and chilled, covered.

Picnic on the Beach

Marinated Black and Green Olives

Crudités with Ravigote Mayonnaise

**Provençale Sandwiches with Tuna,
Basil, and Tomato**

Butter-Rich Fudge Brownies

Antinori's Galestro 1994

Serves 6

Marinated Black and Green Olives

2 cups small green olives
(preferably *picholine**)

2 cups brine-cured black olives
(preferably Niçoise**)

2 small onions, cut into 1/2-inch slices

1/3 cup red-wine vinegar

2 bay leaves

12 fresh thyme sprigs or
1 1/2 teaspoons dried, crumbled

1 teaspoon fennel seeds, crushed lightly
with flat side of a knife

freshly ground black pepper to taste

2 cups olive oil

*available at specialty foods shops

In 2 saucepans of boiling water blanch green
and black olives separately 1 minute and drain in
2 sieves. Divide onions between two 1-quart glass
jars with tight-fitting lids and while still warm pack
green and black olives into separate jars. Divide
vinegar, bay leaves, thyme, fennel seeds, and
pepper between jars, packing fresh thyme down
if necessary. Divide oil between jars and seal jars
with lids. *Marinate olives in a cool, dark place, shaking jars daily, 3 days. Olives keep, covered and chilled, indefinitely.* Makes 4 cups.

Photo on page 44

Crudités with Ravigote Mayonnaise

1 cup mayonnaise

2 hard-cooked large egg yolks,
forced through a sieve

1/4 cup minced fresh parsley leaves

3 tablespoons minced fresh chives

2 tablespoons minced drained bottled capers

1 teaspoon fresh lemon juice, or to taste

1 yellow bell pepper, cut into 1/2-inch strips

1 red bell pepper, cut into 1/2-inch strips

1 cucumber, seeded and cut into
1/2-inch spears

In a bowl combine well mayonnaise, yolks,
parsley, chives, capers, lemon juice, and salt and
pepper to taste. *Ravigote mayonnaise may be made
2 days ahead and chilled, covered.*

Serve bell peppers and cucumber with
mayonnaise. Serves 6.

Photo on page 44

Provençale Sandwiches with Tuna, Basil, and Tomato

1/2	cup red-wine vinegar
6	flat anchovy fillets, rinsed, patted dry, and minced
2	garlic cloves, minced
1	cup extra-virgin olive oil
2	8-inch round loaves crusty bread
2	cups thinly sliced radish
2	cups loosely packed fresh basil leaves
1	cup minced onion, soaked in cold water for 10 minutes and drained well
2	6 1/2-ounce cans tuna in oil, drained and flaked
4	vine-ripened tomatoes (about 1 1/2 pounds), sliced thin

In a bowl whisk together vinegar, anchovies, garlic, and salt and pepper to taste. Add oil in a stream, whisking, and whisk until emulsified. Halve breads horizontally and hollow out halves, leaving ½-inch-thick shells. Spoon one fourth of dressing evenly into each half.

Working with one loaf at a time, arrange half of radish in one bottom shell and top with one fourth of basil. Sprinkle half of onion over basil. Arrange half of tuna on onion and top with one third of remaining basil. Arrange half of tomatoes on basil and fit top shell over tomatoes. Assemble another sandwich in same manner with remaining bread, radish, basil, onion, tuna, and tomatoes. Wrap sandwiches in plastic wrap and put in a shallow baking pan. Top sandwiches with a baking sheet and a large bowl filled with several 2-pound weights and chill 1 hour. *Sandwiches may be made 4 hours ahead and chilled, covered.*

Serve chilled sandwiches cut into wedges. Serves 6.

Photo on page 44

Butter-Rich Fudge Brownies

4	ounces unsweetened chocolate
2	sticks (1 cup) unsalted butter, softened
2	cups sugar
3	large eggs
1	teaspoon vanilla
1	cup sifted all-purpose flour
3/4	cup chopped walnuts

Preheat oven to 350° F. and butter and flour a baking pan, 13- by 9- by 2-inches.

In a small heavy saucepan melt chocolate and 1 stick butter over low heat, stirring, and cool completely. In a large bowl with an electric mixer beat together remaining stick butter and sugar until light and fluffy. Add eggs, 1 at a time, beating well after each addition, and stir in chocolate mixture and vanilla. Add flour and a pinch salt, stirring until blended well, and stir in walnuts.

Pour batter into prepared baking pan, smoothing top, and bake in middle of oven 30 to 40 minutes, or until it pulls away slightly from sides of pan and a tester comes out with crumbs adhering to it. Cool brownie mixture completely before cutting into squares. *Brownies may be made 3 days ahead and kept at room temperature, covered.*

After a nice long day at the beach, you can relax with an alfresco dinner where *everything*, from entrée to dessert, is cooked on the grill! The chicken drumsticks are tenderized in a zesty marinade and brushed with a sweet orange glaze. For an easy side dish, assorted vegetables are served with a summery basil mayonnaise. Then, for a unique finale, nectarines and plums are glazed with honey, sprinkled with red pepper, and served with vanilla ice cream. You may want to grill the fruit before the chicken to avoid having it pick up meat flavors. If so, keep the fruit warm in a flameproof pan or casserole on a cool part of the grill.

Make-Ahead Information

- Basil mayonnaise for the Grilled Vegetables with Basil Mayonnaise may be made 1 day ahead and chilled, covered.
- Chicken for the Grilled Orange Chicken Drumsticks *must* be marinated 1 to 3 hours ahead, covered and chilled.

Saturday-Evening Cookout

Grilled Orange Chicken Drumsticks

Grilled Vegetables with Basil Mayonnaise

Spicy Grilled Nectarines and Plums

Murphy-Goode Alexander Valley
Pinot Blanc 1993

Serves 6

Grilled Orange Chicken Drumsticks

For marinade
3/4 cup fresh orange juice
1/2 cup plain yogurt
1 large garlic clove, minced
1/4 teaspoon cayenne
1/4 cup vegetable oil

12 chicken drumsticks (about 3 1/2 pounds)
For orange glaze
1/2 cup sweet orange marmalade
2 tablespoons fresh orange juice
2 tablespoons fresh rosemary leaves, minced

Make marinade:
In a bowl stir together orange juice, yogurt, garlic, cayenne, and salt and pepper to taste and whisk in oil.

In a large shallow dish arrange chicken, pricked in several places with a fork, in one layer and pour marinade over it. Marinate chicken, covered and chilled, turning once, at least 1 hour and up to 3 hours.

Make orange glaze:
In a small saucepan stir together glaze ingredients and a pinch salt and heat over moderately low heat, stirring, until marmalade is melted. Keep glaze warm, covered.

Prepare grill or heat an oiled ridged grill pan over moderately high heat.

Transfer chicken with tongs to an oiled rack set 5 to 6 inches over glowing coals or to grill pan and grill it, basting with marinade 20 minutes (discard any remaining marinade). Turn chicken over and grill 10 minutes more, or until just cooked through. Brush chicken with orange glaze and grill 3 minutes more, turning it. Serves 6.

Grilled Vegetables with Basil Mayonnaise

For basil mayonnaise
1 cup mayonnaise
1 to 2 teaspoons fresh lemon juice
3/4 cup packed fresh basil leaves

4 carrots including 1 inch of green tops
2 red onions
2 yellow squash
8 radishes including 1/2 inch of green tops
8 small vine-ripened tomatoes including stems
1 red bell pepper, quartered and ribs and seeds discarded
1 yellow or green bell pepper, quartered and ribs and seeds discarded
2 red or yellow Italian sweet peppers, halved lengthwise and ribs and seeds discarded
1/4 pound small okra (about 8)
2 heads Bibb lettuce, halved lengthwise
  olive or vegetable oil for brushing vegetables

Make basil mayonnaise:
In a small bowl stir together mayonnaise, lemon juice, and basil. *Basil mayonnaise may be made 1 day ahead and chilled, covered.*

Prepare grill.

In a large saucepan of boiling salted water cook carrots and onions 5 minutes and transfer with a slotted spoon to a colander. Refresh carrots and onions under cold water and pat dry with paper towels. In boiling salted water cook squash 1 minute. Add radishes and cook 3 minutes. Drain squash and radishes in colander and refresh under cold water. Pat squash and radishes dry with paper towels. Halve onions and squash lengthwise. Brush carrots, onions, squash, radishes, and remaining ingredients with oil. Arrange vegetables in a grill basket and close top of basket, adjusting for size of vegetables. Grill vegetables on a rack set 5 to 6 inches over glowing coals, turning basket once, 5 to 8 minutes, or until tender.

Serve vegetables with basil mayonnaise. Serves 6.

Photo on page 48

Spicy Grilled Nectarines and Plums

3	tablespoons honey
1 1/2	tablespoons fresh lime juice
1/2	teaspoon dried hot red pepper flakes plus additional for sprinkling fruit
3	firm-ripe plums, halved and pitted
3	firm-ripe nectarines, halved and pitted
2	tablespoons unsalted butter, melted

Accompaniment: vanilla ice cream

Prepare grill.

In a small saucepan heat honey, lime juice, and ½ teaspoon red pepper flakes over low heat, stirring, 3 minutes.

Brush cut sides of fruit with butter and grill, cut sides down, on oiled rack set 5 to 6 inches over glowing coals 2 minutes, or until grill marks just show. Turn fruit and brush cut sides with honey glaze. Grill fruit 2 minutes more, or until just softened and heated through. Sprinkle fruit with additional red pepper flakes, if desired.

Serve grilled fruit with vanilla ice cream. Serves 6.

On Sunday, your guests may choose to sit out on the deck, sip a glass of wine, and wait for a cool breeze. Whatever your plans, gather everyone at lunchtime for a light salmon salad drizzled with a lively mustard dressing. For dessert, bring out our unforgettable Frozen Nectarine Mousse with Blackberry Swirl. Use only the freshest fruit for this impressive treat. Look for firm, highly colored, velvet-skinned nectarines and let them ripen for 2 to 3 days at room temperature. Blackberries should be jet black, plump, and dry. Since they are highly perishable, they should be refrigerated immediately and used within 2 to 3 days of purchase.

Make-Ahead Information

- Frozen Nectarine Mousse with Blackberry Swirl: Blackberry mixture may be made 3 days ahead and chilled, covered. Nectarine purée may be made 1 day ahead and chilled, covered. Complete mousse *must* be frozen at least 8 hours and up to 3 days.

Lunch on the Deck

Salmon, Red Onion, and Cucumber Salad with Coriander

Frozen Nectarine Mousse with Blackberry Swirl

Chappellet Vineyard Napa Valley Old Vine Cuvée 1992

Serves 6

Salmon, Red Onion, and Cucumber Salad with Coriander

1 tablespoon plus 1 teaspoon salt
6 Kirby cucumbers or 1 seedless cucumber
1 2-pound piece salmon fillet, seasoned with salt and pepper
2 tablespoons olive oil plus additional for brushing salmon
1/4 cup fresh orange juice
1/4 cup fresh lime juice
1 teaspoon Dijon mustard
1 tablespoon white-wine vinegar
1 1/2 cups minced red onion
1 tablespoon minced garlic
1/3 cup finely chopped fresh coriander
soft-leafed lettuce leaves for lining plates

Accompaniment: thin slices of French or Italian bread, toasted

In a bowl dissolve 1 tablespoon salt in 1 quart cold water. Quarter cucumber lengthwise and cut crosswise into ⅛-inch slices. Add cucumber to water and chill 30 minutes.

Preheat oven to 400° F. and grease a large shallow baking pan.

In prepared pan arrange salmon, skin side down, in one layer and brush with additional oil. Bake salmon in middle of oven 10 to 15 minutes, or until just cooked through. Cool salmon to lukewarm and in a bowl flake into pieces. Drain cucumbers well.

In another bowl whisk together citrus juices, remaining 2 tablespoons oil, mustard, vinegar, remaining 1 teaspoon salt, onion, garlic, coriander, and pepper to taste. Add salmon and cucumbers and toss salad well.

Line 6 plates with lettuce. Divide salad among plates and serve with toast. Serves 6.

Frozen Nectarine Mousse with Blackberry Swirl

    3   cups picked-over blackberries, rinsed
        and drained well
  1/4   cup light corn syrup
  1/4   cup brandy
1 1/2   teaspoons cornstarch, dissolved in
        1 tablespoon cold water
  3/4   pound nectarines, pitted and chopped
    2   teaspoons fresh lemon juice
    1   cup sugar
  1/2   cup water
    4   large eggs
    1   cup well-chilled heavy cream

Garnish: blackberries, fresh mint sprigs, and non-toxic flowers

In a blender or food processor purée blackberries with corn syrup. Strain purée through a fine sieve into a heavy saucepan and simmer, stirring occasionally, 10 minutes, or until reduced to about 1½ cups. Stir in brandy and cornstarch mixture and boil, stirring constantly, 1 minute. Cool mixture to room temperature. *Blackberry mixture may be made 3 days ahead and chilled, covered.*

In a heavy saucepan combine nectarines, lemon juice, ¼ cup sugar, and water and simmer, stirring occasionally, 10 to 15 minutes, or until liquid is reduced to about ¼ cup and nectarines are very soft. In blender or food processor purée nectarine mixture and cool. *Nectarine purée may be made 1 day ahead and chilled, covered.*

In a large metal bowl set over simmering water whisk eggs with remaining ¾ cup sugar until mixture quadruples in volume and registers 160° F. on a candy thermometer and cool. In another bowl whisk cream until it just holds stiff peaks and fold into egg mixture. Fold in nectarine purée gently but thoroughly and pour into an 8½-inch springform pan. Freeze mousse, covered loosely, 45 minutes, or until thickened. Spoon blackberry mixture decoratively over mousse, especially around edge (some will sink into mousse) and draw a skewer or knife through mousse, forming decorative swirls. *Freeze mousse, its surface covered with plastic wrap, at least 8 hours and up to 3 days.*

Just before serving, wrap a dampened kitchen towel around side of pan and remove side. Transfer mousse to a serving plate and garnish with blackberries, mint sprigs, and flowers.

Photo on page 52

A light and easy pasta dinner with flavors from the garden is a perfect way to satisfy your guests before their ride home. The tasty brochettes combine marinated mozzarella with sun-dried tomatoes, onions, and fresh basil and can be assembled hours ahead. And, while you are in the garden picking basil for the brochettes, snip some fresh parsley, mint, chives, coriander, thyme, tarragon, marjoram, or whatever other herbs you have on hand for the entrée — a quick spaghetti dish generously flavored with these aromatic ingredients. Refreshing Caramel Peach Sorbet and buttery Pine Nut Cookies make a sweet, casual finale.

Make-Ahead Information

- Pine Nut Cookies may be made 3 days ahead and kept in an airtight container.

- Mozzarella for the Marinated Mozzarella and Sun-Dried Tomato Brochettes *must* be marinated at least 4 hours ahead at room temperature or chilled, overnight. The brochettes may be assembled 4 hours ahead and chilled, covered.

- Caramel Peach Sorbet *must* be frozen 2 to 3 hours ahead. Additional attention is required during this time.

Send-Off Dinner

Marinated Mozzarella and
Sun-Dried Tomato Brochettes

Spaghetti with Handfuls of Herbs

Caramel Peach Sorbet

Pine Nut Cookies

Atlas Peak Napa Valley Sangiovese 1992

Serves 6

Marinated Mozzarella and Sun-Dried Tomato Brochettes

3/4 pound fresh or smoked mozzarella, cut into 1/2-inch cubes (about 2 cups)
1/4 cup extra-virgin olive oil
1 garlic clove, minced
1 tablespoon white-wine vinegar
1 teaspoon dried basil leaves, crumbled
1/4 teaspoon dried thyme, crumbled
25 sun-dried tomatoes (not packed in oil, about 1 1/2 ounces)
50 small cocktail onions, drained
50 wooden picks
50 fresh basil leaves

In a bowl or resealable heavy plastic bag combine mozzarella, oil, garlic, vinegar, dried herbs, and salt and pepper to taste. *Marinate mozzarella at room temperature at least 4 hours or chilled overnight.*

Soak sun-dried tomatoes in hot water to cover 5 minutes and drain well. Halve tomatoes lengthwise. Wrap 1 tomato half around 1 cocktail onion and thread onto wooden pick with 1 mozzarella cube wrapped in 1 fresh basil leaf. Make more brochettes in same manner with remaining ingredients. *Brochettes may be made 4 hours ahead and chilled, covered.*

Serve brochettes at room temperature. Makes 50 hors d'oeuvres.

Spaghetti with Handfuls of Herbs

1 1/2 cups fresh bread crumbs
3 tablespoons olive oil
3 cups chopped or shredded assorted fresh herb leaves such as parsley, basil, mint, chives, coriander, thyme, tarragon, sorrel, lovage, marjoram, and summer savory
6 small shallots, chopped fine
1/3 cup extra-virgin olive oil
3/4 stick (6 tablespoons) unsalted butter, cut into bits
1 1/2 pounds spaghetti

Bring a kettle of salted water to a boil for pasta.

In a large skillet cook bread crumbs in olive oil over moderate heat, stirring, until golden and crisp and transfer to a small bowl. In a large serving bowl combine herbs, shallots, extra-virgin olive oil, and butter. In kettle of boiling water cook pasta until *al dente*. Drain pasta and add to herb mixture, tossing to coat well. Season pasta with salt and pepper and sprinkle with bread crumbs. Serves 6.

Photo on page 56

Caramel Peach Sorbet

2/3 cup sugar
3 cups canned peach nectar

Accompaniment: sliced peaches

In a dry large deep heavy skillet cook sugar over moderately high heat, stirring constantly with a fork, until melted completely and a deep golden caramel. Add nectar carefully (mixture will bubble up) and cook, stirring, until caramel is completely dissolved. Cool mixture.

Transfer mixture to 2 metal ice-cube trays without dividers or a shallow metal pan and freeze, stirring and crushing lumps with a fork every 30 minutes, 2 to 3 hours, or until firm but not frozen hard. Scrape sorbet with a fork to lighten texture if necessary.

Scoop sorbet into goblets and serve with sliced peaches. Makes about 1½ quarts.

Pine Nut Cookies

1 1/2 sticks (3/4 cup) unsalted butter, softened
1/2 cup firmly packed light brown sugar
1/2 cup granulated sugar
1 large egg
1 teaspoon vanilla
1/8 teaspoon almond extract
1 1/2 cups all-purpose flour
3/4 teaspoon baking powder
1/2 teaspoon salt
1/4 cup pine nuts

In a bowl with an electric mixer beat butter with sugars until light and fluffy and beat in egg, vanilla, and almond extract. Into egg mixture sift together flour, baking powder, and salt and beat until combined well. Chill dough 1 hour, or until firm enough to handle.

Halve dough and on a sheet of wax paper form each half into a 6-inch log, using wax paper as a guide. *Chill logs, wrapped in wax paper, at least 4 hours or overnight.*

Preheat oven to 350° F. and lightly butter 2 baking sheets.

Cut logs into ¼-inch slices with a sharp knife and arrange 3 inches apart on prepared baking sheets. Press a few pine nuts onto each cookie. Bake cookies in batches in middle of oven 10 to 12 minutes, or until golden, and cool on baking sheets 1 minute. Transfer cookies to racks and cool completely. *Cookies may be made 3 days ahead and kept in an airtight container.* Makes about 48 cookies.

fall

foliage

weekend

Autumn leaves, in an array of gold, red, and orange hues, paint a spectacular picture. By the time nature's breathtaking display is at its peak, there is an invigorating nip in the air and pumpkin patches and apple orchards are packed with seasonal harvests, ready for eager pickers. The countryside beckons, and our delightful apple-picking picnic ensures a perfect day. It's all planned — along with an entire weekend of warming fall menus.

Bring your guests in from a chilly evening to the warmth of a casual dinner of comforting dishes. Topped with crunchy Parmesan bread crumbs, our macaroni and cheese combines mild Monterey Jack and extra-sharp Cheddar in a spicy tomato sauce; an herbed lentil salad served on a bed of bitter escarole makes a tasty accompaniment. For dessert, sautéed pears are a simple yet special finale, with a *crème de cassis* and red currant jelly sauce, toasted almonds, and a dollop of whipped cream. Use Comice or Bartlett pears for maximum flavor. The fruit should be bought when firm, allowed to ripen at room temperature, then refrigerated.

Make-Ahead Information

- Spicy Macaroni and Cheese may be prepared, in part, 1 day ahead and chilled, covered. Allow an additional 30 minutes to finalize.

- Lentils for Lentil Salad with Escarole may be prepared, in part, 1 day ahead and chilled, covered.

A Welcoming Fall Dinner

Spicy Macaroni and Cheese

Lentil Salad with Escarole

Sautéed Pears with Currant Sauce

Kunde Vallée de la Lune 1992

Serves 6

Spicy Macaroni and Cheese

1 1/2	cups finely chopped onion
2	large garlic cloves, minced
1 1/2	tablespoons minced pickled *jalapeño* chilies, or to taste
1	teaspoon ground coriander
1 1/2	teaspoons ground cumin
1/2	stick (1/4 cup) unsalted butter
1/4	cup all-purpose flour
4	cups milk
1	28-ounce can plum tomatoes, juice discarded and tomatoes chopped and drained well
	cayenne to taste
1	pound elbow macaroni
1 1/2	cups coarsely grated Monterey Jack cheese (about 6 ounces)
1 1/2	cups coarsely grated extra-sharp Cheddar cheese (about 6 ounces)
1 1/2	cups fresh bread crumbs
1 1/3	cups freshly grated Parmesan cheese (about 1/4 pound)

Preheat oven to 375° F. and butter a 13- by 9-inch shallow baking dish or a 3-quart gratin dish.

Bring a kettle of salted water to a boil for macaroni.

In a large heavy saucepan cook onion, garlic, *jalapeños*, coriander, and cumin in butter over moderately low heat, stirring, until onion is softened. Stir in flour and cook, stirring, 3 minutes. Add milk in a stream, whisking. Bring liquid to a boil, whisking, and whisk in tomatoes. Simmer mixture 2 minutes and add cayenne and salt and pepper to taste.

In boiling water cook macaroni 6 minutes, or until barely *al dente*, and drain well. In a large bowl combine macaroni with tomato mixture and stir in Monterey Jack and Cheddar. Transfer mixture to prepared dish. *Macaroni and cheese may be prepared up to this point 1 day ahead and chilled, covered.* In a bowl stir together bread crumbs and Parmesan and sprinkle evenly over macaroni. Bake macaroni and cheese in middle of oven 20 to 25 minutes, or until golden and bubbling. Serves 6.

Photo on page 62

Lentil Salad with Escarole

1/2 pound lentils (about 1 1/2 cups)
2 cups low-salt chicken broth
1 cup water
1/2 teaspoon dried oregano, crumbled
1/2 teaspoon dried basil, crumbled
1/2 teaspoon dried thyme, crumbled
1 bay leaf
6 tablespoons olive oil
4 tablespoons fresh lemon juice
1 teaspoon salt
3 celery ribs, sliced thin
1 medium red onion, chopped fine
1/3 cup chopped fresh flat-leafed parsley
1 head escarole (about 3/4 pound)

In a stainless-steel or enameled saucepan combine lentils, broth, water, dried herbs, and bay leaf. Bring liquid to a boil and simmer, covered, 20 minutes, or until lentils are tender.

Drain lentils in a sieve and discard bay leaf. In a bowl stir together 4 tablespoons oil, 3 tablespoons lemon juice, salt, and pepper to taste and stir into lentils. *Lentil salad may be prepared up to this point 1 day ahead and chilled, covered.* Stir in celery, onion, and parsley.

Cut escarole into ¼-inch strips and in bowl toss with remaining 2 tablespoons oil and 1 tablespoon lemon juice and salt and pepper to taste.

Line 6 salad plates with escarole and mound lentil salad on top. Serves 6.

Sautéed Pears with Currant Sauce

6 firm-ripe pears
2 tablespoons fresh lemon juice
1/2 stick (1/4 cup) unsalted butter
1/4 cup *crème de cassis*
1/2 cup red currant jelly
1/4 cup slivered blanched almonds, toasted lightly

Accompaniment: whipped cream

Peel and core pears and cut into eighths. In a bowl toss pears with lemon juice.

In a stainless-steel or enameled skillet heat butter over moderately high heat and sauté pears, stirring, 2 minutes. Cook pears, covered, over low heat, stirring occasionally, until just tender, 3 to 5 minutes. With a slotted spoon divide pears among 6 dessert plates. To skillet add *crème de cassis* and jelly and cook over moderately high heat, stirring, until jelly is melted and sauce is syrupy.

Spoon currant sauce over pears and sprinkle with almonds. Serve pears with whipped cream. Serves 6.

Our apple-picking picnic offers an extra-special way to enjoy the foliage. Almost everything in this menu can be made ahead, so you'll be able to get an early start. At the orchard, be selective — choose only firm, unblemished apples. (And, if you plan to bake a pie, look for varieties that hold their shape, such as Golden Delicious.) After filling a bushel or two, find a pretty spot to unpack your feast: rich Stilton soup; smoked turkey sandwiches with chutney and curried mayonnaise; and zesty Caraway Celery Slaw. Two delightful sorbets and Oatmeal Cinnamon Tuiles follow. At home, be sure to refrigerate your apples to keep them crisp and juicy.

Make-Ahead Information

- Stilton Soup with Sherry and Hazelnuts may be made, in part, 2 days ahead. Allow an additional 10 minutes to finalize.

- Dressing for the Caraway Celery Slaw may be made 2 days ahead and chilled, covered.

- Apple Sorbet and Caramel Sorbet may be made 1 week ahead.

- Oatmeal Cinnamon Tuiles may be made 1 day ahead and kept in an airtight container.

An Apple-Picking Picnic

Stilton Soup with Sherry and Hazelnuts

Curried Smoked Turkey Sandwiches

Caraway Celery Slaw

Apple Sorbet and Caramel Sorbet

Oatmeal Cinnamon Tuiles

Wyder's Dry Draft
Fermented Canadian Cider
and
Trefethen Napa Valley
Dry Riesling 1993

Serves 6

Stilton Soup with Sherry and Hazelnuts

1 1/2 cups finely chopped celery
1 large onion, chopped fine
1 large garlic clove, minced
1 bay leaf
1/2 teaspoon dried thyme, crumbled
2 tablespoons unsalted butter
2 russet (baking) potatoes (about 1 pound)
2 cups low-salt chicken broth
1 cup water
1 cup half-and-half
6 ounces Stilton cheese, crumbled
(about 1 1/2 cups)
3 tablespoons medium-dry Sherry, or to taste

Garnish: 3 tablespoons toasted hazelnuts, chopped

In a large saucepan cook celery, onion, and garlic with bay leaf and thyme in butter over moderate heat, stirring, 5 minutes, or until vegetables are softened. Peel potatoes and slice thin. Add potatoes to vegetables with broth and water and simmer, covered, 15 minutes, or until potatoes are very tender. Discard bay leaf and in a blender purée soup in batches. Transfer purée to cleaned pan and stir in half-and-half. *Soup may be prepared up to this point 2 days ahead and cooled completely before chilling, covered.* Heat soup over low heat, whisking, and add Stilton, whisking until cheese is melted and soup is smooth. Whisk in Sherry and salt and pepper to taste. (Do not let soup boil.)

Serve soup garnished with hazelnuts. Makes about 7½ cups.

Caraway Celery Slaw

For dressing
1/4 cup Dijon mustard
1/4 cup half-and-half
1 large whole egg plus 1 large egg yolk
3 tablespoons white-wine vinegar
2 teaspoons caraway seeds
1/4 cup olive oil

2 pounds celery, sliced thin (about 8 cups)
3/4 pound finely shredded white cabbage
(about 4 cups)
1 medium onion, minced
1/2 cup thinly sliced bottled pimiento or
roasted red pepper, drained

Make dressing:
In a stainless-steel or enameled saucepan cook mustard, half-and-half, whole egg, yolk, vinegar, caraway seeds, and salt and pepper to taste over moderately low heat, whisking, until thickened slightly. Remove pan from heat and add oil in a stream, whisking. *Dressing may be made 2 days ahead and chilled, covered.*

In a large bowl combine remaining ingredients and toss with dressing and salt and pepper to taste. Chill slaw, covered, 1 hour. Serves 6.

Curried Smoked Turkey Sandwiches

1/3 cup mayonnaise
1/3 cup bottled mango chutney, or to taste,
any large pieces chopped
1 to 2 tablespoons minced fresh
parsley leaves
2 teaspoons curry powder, or to taste
fresh lemon juice to taste
2 loaves Italian or French bread
(each about 15 inches long), cut into thirds
and halved horizontally
1 pound thinly sliced smoked turkey breast
watercress sprigs, coarse stems discarded

In a small bowl stir together mayonnaise, chutney, parsley to taste, curry powder, lemon juice, and salt and pepper to taste until combined well. Spread each bread half with 1 tablespoon chutney mixture and divide turkey among bottom halves of bread. Top turkey with watercress and cover with top halves of bread. Makes 6 sandwiches.

Oatmeal Cinnamon Tuiles

    2 tablespoons unsalted butter, softened
  1/4 cup sugar
  1/4 teaspoon vanilla
  1/4 teaspoon cinnamon
  1/4 teaspoon salt
    1 large egg white
    2 tablespoons all-purpose flour
  1/4 cup old-fashioned rolled oats

Preheat oven to 425° F. and generously butter 2 large baking sheets.

In a small bowl beat together with a wooden spoon butter, sugar, vanilla, cinnamon, and salt. Add white and whisk until smooth. Sift in flour and stir in oats thoroughly. Drop batter by rounded teaspoons 4 inches apart onto prepared baking sheets. With back of wooden spoon spread batter into 2½-inch rounds and bake in batches in middle of oven 4 to 6 minutes, or until edges are golden. Immediately transfer *tuiles* with a metal spatula to a rolling pin and cool in curved shapes. Tuiles *may be made 1 day ahead and kept in an airtight container.* Makes about 12 *tuiles.*

Photo on page 66

Apple Sorbet

    2 cups clear apple juice
    3 Granny Smith apples (about 1 1/2 pounds),
       peeled and cut into 1/2-inch pieces
    1 tablespoon fresh lemon juice
    3 tablespoons sugar

In a large saucepan combine all ingredients and a pinch salt and simmer, uncovered, 10 minutes, or until apples are very tender. Strain mixture through a sieve into a blender and add half of solids in sieve to blender, discarding remaining solids. Purée apple mixture and chill, covered, until cold. Freeze sorbet in an ice-cream maker. *Sorbet may be made 1 week ahead.* Makes 3 cups.

Photo on page 66

Caramel Sorbet

    1 cup granulated sugar
    2 cups water
  1/4 teaspoon salt
    1 teaspoon vanilla

In a dry heavy saucepan cook granulated sugar over moderate heat, without stirring, until it begins to melt and continue to cook, stirring with a fork, until melted completely and a deep caramel. Remove pan from heat and carefully add water down side of pan. Return pan to heat and cook caramel, stirring, until dissolved completely. Stir in salt and vanilla and chill, covered, until cold. Freeze sorbet in an ice-cream maker. *Sorbet may be made 1 week ahead.* Makes about 3 cups.

Photo on page 66

A full day outdoors in the country is bound to increase everyone's appetite, so we planned our dinner tonight to be exceptionally hearty. We begin with a flavorful salad of spinach, goat cheese, and bacon tossed in a citrus dressing. (Pre-washed and stemmed bagged spinach may be used to save time – just make sure it is top-quality.) Then, tender peppercorn steaks in a creamy Cognac sauce are accompanied by Fried Shoestring Potatoes (use russets for ideal size and texture) and Herbed Tomatoes. Dreamy Chocolate Crèmes Brûlées follow, perhaps a bit later, when everyone is ready to indulge once again.

Make-Ahead Information

- Steak for Steak with Peppercorns *must* stand at room temperature, pressed with pepper and covered, for 1 hour before proceeding with recipe.

- Fried Shoestring Potatoes may be made 8 hours ahead and kept in an airtight container.

- Tomatoes for Herbed Tomatoes may be made, in part, 1 day ahead and chilled, covered. Bread crumb mixture may be made 1 day ahead and kept in an airtight container at room temperature. Allow approximately 10 minutes to finalize.

- Chocolate Crèmes Brûlées: Custard *must* stand at room temperature for 1 hour before baking; Baked custards may be made, in part, 2 days ahead and chilled, covered. Allow approximately 25 minutes to finalize.

A Hearty Autumn Dinner

Spinach, Goat Cheese, and Bacon Salad with Orange Pecan Dressing

Steak with Peppercorns

Fried Shoestring Potatoes

Herbed Tomatoes

Chocolate Crèmes Brûlées

Sterling Vineyards Winery Lake, Napa Valley Pinot Noir 1992

Serves 6

Spinach, Goat Cheese, and Bacon Salad with Orange Pecan Dressing

- 8 cups firmly packed spinach leaves (about 1 pound with stems), washed well, spun dry, and torn into pieces
- 1/3 cup crumbled mild goat cheese
- 6 bacon slices, cooked until crisp and crumbled
- 1/2 small red onion, sliced thin
  For dressing
- 1 navel orange, rind and pith cut away with a serrated knife and fruit cut into sections
- 1/4 cup pecans, toasted lightly
- 2 teaspoons red-wine vinegar
- 1/8 teaspoon cayenne
- 1/2 cup olive oil

In a large bowl toss together spinach, goat cheese, bacon, and onion.

Make dressing:

In a blender blend together orange, pecans, vinegar, cayenne, and salt and pepper to taste until smooth. With motor running add oil in a stream and blend until emulsified.

Pour dressing over salad and toss well. Serves 6.

Steak with Peppercorns

- 4 1/2 tablespoons whole black peppercorns
- 6 1/2-pound boneless shell steaks (each about 3/4 inch thick)
- 2 tablespoons vegetable oil
- 2 tablespoons unsalted butter
- 1/3 cup minced shallot
- 2/3 cup Cognac
- 1 1/2 cups beef broth
- 1 cup heavy cream

Garnish: watercress sprigs

In a heavy-duty sealable plastic bag or between 2 sheets of wax paper crush peppercorns coarse with bottom of a heavy skillet. Pat steaks dry. Press pepper into both sides of steaks and let stand at room temperature, covered loosely with wax paper, 1 hour.

In each of 2 large heavy skillets heat 1 tablespoon oil and 1 tablespoon butter over moderately high heat until foam subsides and sauté steaks, seasoning them with salt, 2 to 2½ minutes on each side, or until just springy to the touch, for medium-rare. Transfer steaks with a slotted spatula to a platter and keep warm, covered loosely.

Pour off almost all fat remaining in 1 skillet. Add shallot and cook over moderate heat, stirring, until softened. Add Cognac and boil until reduced to a glaze. Add broth and boil until reduced by about half. Add cream and boil, stirring occasionally, until slightly thickened. Season sauce with salt.

Garnish steaks with watercress and serve sauce on the side. Serves 6.

Photo on page 70

Fried Shoestring Potatoes

2 1/4 pounds russet (baking) potatoes
       vegetable oil for deep frying

Working with 1 potato at a time, peel potatoes
and put in a large bowl of ice water. With a
mandoline or similar slicing device cut potatoes
lengthwise into thin (⅛-inch-thick) sticks,
dropping them as cut into bowl of water. Stir
potatoes to help wash off excess starch.

Drain potatoes and pat dry thoroughly
between several layers of paper towels. In a deep
fryer fry potatoes in small batches in 2 inches of
380° F. oil, making sure oil returns to 380° F.
before adding each new batch, 1½ to 2 minutes,
or until golden, and transfer with a skimmer or
slotted spoon to folded brown paper bags or
paper towels to drain. Season potatoes with salt.
*Potatoes may be made 8 hours ahead and kept in an
airtight container. Just before serving reheat potatoes in
a large roasting pan in a preheated 325° F. oven until
crisp and hot, 5 to 10 minutes.* Serves 6.

Photo on page 70

Herbed Tomatoes

  6 vine-ripened tomatoes (about 1 1/2 pounds)
1/4 cup olive oil plus additional for
     brushing tomatoes
     For bread crumb mixture
1/2 cup fresh bread crumbs
  1 flat anchovy fillet, rinsed, patted dry,
     and minced
1 1/2 teaspoons minced garlic
1/2 cup freshly grated Parmesan cheese
1/2 cup minced fresh parsley leaves
1/4 cup finely chopped fresh basil leaves

Preheat oven to 325° F. and lightly oil a shallow
baking pan.

Cut off top third of each tomato, discarding
it, and scoop out seeds with a small spoon. Brush
outside of tomatoes with additional oil and arrange
tomatoes, cut sides up, on prepared baking pan.
Season insides of tomatoes with salt and pepper
and bake in oven 20 minutes. Invert tomatoes
onto paper towels and drain 15 minutes. *Tomatoes
may be prepared up to this point 1 day ahead and
chilled, covered.*

Make bread crumb mixture:
In a small bowl toss together bread crumb
mixture ingredients and salt and pepper to taste.
*Bread crumb mixture may be made 1 day ahead and
kept in an airtight container at room temperature.*

Preheat broiler.
Divide bread crumb mixture among
baked tomatoes, making sure cavities are filled
and mounding mixture, and drizzle with remaining ¼ cup oil. Broil tomatoes on baking pan
under broiler about 4 inches from heat 2 to 4
minutes, or until topping is crisp and golden
brown. Serves 6.

Photo on page 70

Chocolate Crèmes Brûlées

    1 cup milk
    1 cup half-and-half
    4 ounces fine-quality bittersweet
       chocolate, chopped fine
    1 cup heavy cream
    6 large egg yolks
  1/2 cup granulated sugar
    6 tablespoons firmly packed light
       brown sugar

In a saucepan scald milk and half-and-half over
moderate heat and add chocolate, stirring until
melted. Remove pan from heat and stir in cream.
In a bowl whisk together yolks and granulated
sugar until combined well. Add chocolate mixture
in a slow stream, whisking constantly, and strain
through a very fine sieve into another bowl. Let
custard stand at room temperature 1 hour and
skim off any foam.

Preheat oven to 250° F.

Pour ⅔ cup custard slowly into each of
six 6-inch round (1-inch deep) flameproof dishes.
Bake custards in middle of oven 25 to 30 minutes,
or until just set but tremble slightly. Cool custards
and chill until cold. *Custards may be prepared up to
this point 2 days ahead and chilled, covered.*

Preheat broiler.

Sift 1 tablespoon brown sugar evenly over
each custard and broil about 3 inches from heat
until brown sugar is melted and caramelized, 1 to 3
minutes. Chill *crèmes brûlées* 20 minutes, or until
cold. Serves 6.

What could be more enticing than the sweet aroma of apple pie bubbling in the oven on a chilly day? After yesterday's outing, you'll have plenty of juicy apples on hand for today's luncheon finale. In fact, you may want to make a second pie while you're at it! Our light soup-and-salad meal is a potpourri of goodness from the garden — onion, garlic, celery, carrots, turnips, red potatoes, spinach, *arugula*, and *frisée* all appear. (Buy only firm, fresh vegetables and crisp greens, and remember that small turnips have the best flavor.) Our fanciful salad is served with a warm vinaigrette, a lovely touch for cool weather.

Make-Ahead Information

- White Bean and Vegetable Soup may be prepared, in part, 3 days ahead. Allow approximately 15 minutes to finalize.

- Shell for Apple and Pecan Crisp Pie may be made 1 day ahead and covered, chilled.

Lunch for a Chilly Day

White Bean and Vegetable Soup

Arugula and Frisée Salad

Apple and Pecan Crisp Pie

Nippozano Chianti Rufina Riserva 1989, Marchesi de' Frescobaldi

for dessert,
Renaissance Late Harvest
North Yuba Sauvignon Blanc 1991

Serves 6

White Bean and Vegetable Soup

1/4   pound salt pork, rind discarded and meat cut into 1/4-inch dice

2   cups finely chopped onion

2   large garlic cloves, minced

1   bay leaf

1   teaspoon dried rosemary, crumbled

1   pound small red potatoes

4   celery ribs, cut crosswise into 1/4-inch slices (about 2 cups)

4   large carrots, cut crosswise into 1/4-inch slices (about 2 cups)

1   pound turnips, peeled and cut into 3/4-inch pieces

1   pound dried white beans such as Great Northern, soaked in cold water to cover by 2 inches overnight or quick-soaked (procedure follows) and drained

4   cups chicken broth plus, if desired, additional for thinning soup

6   cups water

6   cups packed fresh spinach leaves, washed well, spun dry, and shredded coarse

1   cup dry white wine

Accompaniment: freshly grated Parmesan cheese to taste

In a heavy kettle cook salt pork over moderately low heat, stirring, until crisp. Transfer cracklings with a slotted spoon to paper towels and reserve. In fat remaining in kettle cook onion and garlic with bay leaf and rosemary, stirring, until onion is softened. Cut potatoes into 1-inch pieces and add to onion mixture with celery, carrots, turnips, beans, 4 cups broth, and water and simmer, covered, stirring occasionally, 1½ to 2 hours, or until beans are tender. *Soup may be prepared up to this point 3 days ahead and cooled completely before chilling, covered. Return soup to a simmer before proceeding with recipe.* Stir in spinach and simmer, uncovered, 5 minutes, or until spinach is cooked. Stir in wine, enough additional broth to thin soup to desired consistency, and salt and pepper to taste. Discard bay leaf and simmer, stirring, 5 minutes.

Serve soup sprinkled with Parmesan and reserved cracklings. Makes about 12 cups.

Photo on page 76

To Quick Soak Dried Beans

1   pound dried beans, picked over

In a colander rinse beans under cold water and discard any discolored ones. In a kettle combine beans with cold water to cover by 2 inches and bring to a boil. Boil beans 2 minutes. Remove kettle from heat and soak beans, covered, 1 hour.

Arugula and Frisée Salad

2 1/2   tablespoons balsamic vinegar
    1   tablespoon white-wine vinegar
1/2   pound *arugula* (preferably small young
      greens, coarse stems discarded),
      washed well, spun dry, and if necessary
      cut into bite-size pieces
      (about 5 cups loosely packed)
3/4   pound *frisée** (French curly chicory),
      rinsed, spun dry, and cut into bite-size
      pieces (about 6 cups loosely packed)
    5   tablespoons olive oil

*available at specialty produce markets

In a small bowl stir together vinegars and salt to taste. In a large heatproof salad bowl toss together *arugula* and *frisée*. In a small saucepan heat oil over moderate heat until hot but not smoking and drizzle evenly over greens, stirring constantly. Drizzle vinegar mixture evenly over greens, stirring constantly. Serves 6.

Apple and Pecan Crisp Pie

    1   recipe pastry dough (page 23)
      For filling
    2   pounds Golden Delicious apples (about 4)
1/3   cup sugar
1/4   cup finely chopped pecans, toasted lightly
    1   tablespoon all-purpose flour
    1   tablespoon fresh orange juice
3/4   teaspoon freshly grated orange zest
1/2   teaspoon cinnamon
      For streusel
3/4   cup quick-cooking rolled oats
1/3   cup all-purpose flour
1/4   cup firmly packed light brown sugar
1/4   teaspoon salt
1/2   stick (1/4 cup) cold unsalted butter,
      cut into bits

Roll out dough ⅛ inch thick on a lightly floured surface. Fit dough into a 9-inch (1-quart capacity, about 1 inch deep) metal pie plate and crimp edge decoratively. Chill shell 30 minutes. *Shell may be made 1 day ahead and chilled, covered.*

Preheat oven to 375° F.

Make filling:

Peel and core apples and slice thin. In a bowl combine apples with remaining filling ingredients and toss well.

Make streusel:

In a bowl blend streusel ingredients until mixture resembles very coarse meal.

Put filling in shell, packing it slightly, and sprinkle streusel over it. Bake pie in middle of oven 50 to 55 minutes, or until streusel is crisp and golden and fruit is tender when pierced with a skewer. Cool pie in pan on a rack.

Serve pie warm or at room temperature.

winter
ski
weekend

Purple-gray skies herald snow, a sure sign that it is time to take out the skis, pack up the car, and head for the slopes. As the cold winds blow, there is no better season to gather with friends for a cozy weekend. Whether you are skiing, making a snowman, going for a sleigh ride, or simply relaxing by the fire, our winter weekend menus keep you toasty with piping-hot drinks, hearty stews, steaming soups, and comforting desserts. ❄

Traveling in winter weather can be unpredictable. In case all your guests do not arrive promptly, our casual kitchen dinner can be ready when you are. Buttery herbed almonds and pecans and a favorite hot drink will keep early arrivals happy, while the hearty Chicken and Garbanzo Stew can be kept warm until everyone appears. The stew, chili bread, and cupcakes all can be made the day before; the only last-minute dish is the quick wilted spinach salad with warm pear dressing.

Make-Ahead Information

- Chicken and Garbanzo Stew may be made 1 day ahead and chilled, covered. (If you use fresh chick-peas, they will have to soak overnight before being cooked.)

- Beer, Cornmeal, and Chili Quick Bread may be made 1 day ahead and kept wrapped tightly in plastic wrap.

- Cupcakes and icing for Cinnamon Chocolate Cupcakes with Chocolate Icing both may be made 1 day ahead and kept separately—the cupcakes in an airtight container; the icing chilled, covered.

- Butter-Toasted Almonds and Pecans with Herbs may be made 6 hours ahead and kept in an airtight container.

Dinner in a Cozy Kitchen

**Butter-Toasted Almonds
and Pecans with Herbs**

Chicken and Garbanzo Stew

Beer, Cornmeal, and Chili Quick Bread
or **Crusty Bread** (store-bought)

**Wilted Spinach Salad with
Warm Pear and Red Onion Dressing**

**Cinnamon Chocolate Cupcakes
with Chocolate Icing**

Sanford Santa Barbara County Chardonnay 1992

Serves 6

Butter-Toasted Almonds and Pecans with Herbs

5	tablespoons unsalted butter
1	garlic clove, halved lengthwise
1/2	pound blanched almonds (about 2 cups), halved
1/2	pound pecan halves (about 2 1/3 cups)
1/2	teaspoon dried tarragon, crumbled fine
1/2	teaspoon dried rosemary, crumbled fine
	coarse salt to taste

In a large heavy skillet heat butter with garlic over moderately high heat until foam subsides and discard garlic. In butter cook almonds over moderate heat, stirring constantly, 3 to 4 minutes, or until pale golden. Add pecans and dried herbs and cook, stirring constantly, 3 to 4 minutes, or until golden and crisp. Transfer nuts with a slotted spoon to paper towels to drain and sprinkle with coarse salt. Cool nuts completely. *Herbed nuts may be made 6 hours ahead and kept in an airtight container.* Makes about 4⅓ cups.

Chicken and Garbanzo Stew

2	3-pound chickens, cut into serving pieces
2	tablespoons olive oil
1	tablespoon unsalted butter
2	small onions, minced
3	garlic cloves
1 1/2	tablespoons ground cumin
1/2	teaspoon ground ginger
1/2	teaspoon dried hot red pepper flakes
4	cups chicken broth
5	cups cooked chick-peas, or three 1-pound cans, rinsed and drained
1	cup chopped fresh coriander

Pat chicken dry and season with salt and pepper. In a large heavy kettle heat oil and butter over moderately high heat until foam subsides and brown chicken in batches, transferring it as browned to a large bowl. Pour off half of fat in kettle and in remaining fat cook onions, 2 garlic cloves, minced, cumin, ginger, and red pepper flakes over moderately low heat, stirring, until onions are softened.

Return chicken to kettle and add broth and chick-peas. Simmer mixture, covered, 45 minutes. (Mixture will be soupy. If thicker stew is desired, transfer chicken to a bowl and boil mixture until reduced to desired consistency.) Mince remaining garlic clove with coriander and sprinkle over stew. Season stew with salt and pepper. *Stew may be made 1 day ahead and chilled, covered.* Serves 8.

Photo on page 82

Beer, Cornmeal, and Chili Quick Bread

2 3/4	cups all-purpose flour
3/4	cup yellow cornmeal
1	teaspoon salt
1/2	teaspoon baking soda
1 1/2	teaspoons baking powder
1	large egg, beaten lightly
1	12-ounce bottle of beer (not dark)
1	4-ounce can mild green chilies, drained, chopped, and patted dry
1	cup coarsely grated pepper Jack cheese (about 3 ounces)
1/3	cup chopped scallion (white and green parts)
1	tablespoon olive oil

Preheat oven to 350° F. and grease and flour a loaf pan, 9 by 5 by 3 inches, knocking out excess.

In a large bowl whisk together flour, cornmeal, salt, baking soda, and baking powder. Add remaining ingredients and stir until just combined. Turn batter into prepared pan, smoothing top, and bake in middle of oven 45 minutes, or until a tester comes out clean. Turn bread out onto a rack and cool. *Bread may be made 1 day ahead and kept wrapped tightly in plastic wrap.*

Wilted Spinach Salad with Warm Pear and Red Onion Dressing

1/4 cup finely chopped red onion
1/2 cup finely chopped peeled firm-ripe Comice pears
5 tablespoons olive oil
2 tablespoons cider vinegar
1 1/2 cups unpasteurized apple cider
2 teaspoons Dijon mustard
1 1/2 pounds fresh spinach leaves, washed well and spun dry

In a skillet cook onion and pears in 2 tablespoons oil over moderate heat, stirring, 1 minute. Add vinegar, cider, and salt and pepper to taste and boil, stirring occasionally, 6 to 8 minutes, or until reduced to about ¾ cup. Whisk in mustard, remaining 3 tablespoons oil, and salt and pepper to taste. In a large bowl toss spinach with warm dressing until just wilted. Serves 6.

Cinnamon Chocolate Cupcakes with Chocolate Icing

1/3 cup Dutch-process cocoa powder
1/2 cup boiling-hot water
1 cup all-purpose flour
3/4 teaspoon cinnamon
1/2 teaspoon baking soda
1/2 teaspoon salt
3/4 stick (6 tablespoons) unsalted butter, softened
1/2 cup firmly packed light brown sugar
1 whole large egg plus 1 large egg yolk
3/4 cup semisweet chocolate chips
1/4 cup heavy cream

Preheat oven to 350° F. and line twelve ½-cup muffin tins with paper cups.

In a small bowl whisk together cocoa powder and water until cocoa powder is dissolved and cool to room temperature. In a bowl whisk together flour, cinnamon, baking soda, and salt. In another bowl with an electric mixer beat together butter and sugar and add whole egg and yolk, beating until combined well. Beat in cocoa mixture alternately with flour mixture, beating well after each addition, and divide among prepared muffin tins. Bake cupcakes in middle of oven 15 minutes, or until a tester comes out clean. Turn cupcakes out onto a rack and cool completely. *Cupcakes may be made 1 day ahead and kept in an airtight container.*

In a small metal bowl set over a saucepan of barely simmering water melt chips with cream, stirring occasionally, until smooth. Chill icing, stirring occasionally, until firm enough to spread. *Icing may be made 1 day ahead and chilled, covered. Let icing soften to spreading consistency before spreading on cupcakes.* Spread icing on cupcakes. Makes 12 cupcakes.

To enjoy as much time as possible on the slopes, skiers need a quick, satisfying breakfast. Our fast and easy early-morning menu is a perfect little high-carbohydrate meal with staying power. The granola, a crunchy combination of rolled oats, rye, barley, pecans, wheat germ, and dried fruit, can be made weeks ahead, and the scones, heartened with whole-wheat flour, take only minutes to prepare. Plan to get up a bit before your guests so you can serve the scones fresh from the oven. And if you decide to offer steaming hot chocolate, turn to page 205 for a great recipe. For a frothy result, you can blend the beverage in a blender, in batches.

Make-Ahead Information

- Multigrain Granola keeps 4 weeks, in an airtight container, chilled.

Pre-Ski Breakfast

Multigrain Granola

Orange Caraway Scones

Coffee
Tea
Hot Chocolate

Serves 6

Multigrain Granola

3 cups mixed rolled grains such as rolled oats, rye, wheat, and barley*

1/3 cup sesame seeds

1 cup pecan halves or other nutmeats, 1/2 cup chopped and 1/2 cup left whole

1/2 cup honey

1/2 teaspoon pumpkin-pie spice

2 cups mixed dried fruit such as dried sour cherries, diced peaches, diced apricots, diced pears, raisins, currants, and chopped pitted prunes*

1/2 cup toasted wheat germ

*available at natural foods stores and some supermarkets

Preheat oven to 350° F.

In a large shallow baking pan toast rolled grains with sesame seeds in middle of oven, stirring every 3 minutes, for 10 minutes, or until golden. In a large bowl stir together nuts, honey, and pumpkin-pie spice. Stir in hot toasted grain mixture and combine well. Transfer mixture to baking pan, spreading it evenly, and toast in middle of oven, stirring every 3 minutes, for 10 minutes, or until browned. Cool grain and nut mixture completely. In a small bowl toss together dried fruit and wheat germ and stir into grain and nut mixture. *Granola keeps 4 weeks in an airtight container, chilled.* Makes about 8 cups.

Photo on page 86

Orange Caraway Scones

2 large eggs

1/2 cup heavy cream

3 tablespoons fresh orange juice

1 tablespoon freshly grated orange zest

1 1/2 teaspoons caraway seeds

1 1/4 cups all-purpose flour

1/3 cup whole-wheat flour

1/3 cup plus 1 tablespoon sugar

2 3/4 teaspoons baking powder

1 teaspoon salt

Preheat oven to 425° F. and grease a baking sheet.

In a small bowl whisk together eggs and cream, reserving 1 tablespoon egg mixture, and stir in orange juice, zest, and caraway seeds. In a bowl whisk together flours, 1/3 cup sugar, baking powder, and salt. Add orange juice mixture and stir with a fork until a dough just forms (dough will be very sticky). With floured hands knead dough lightly on a floured surface 30 seconds. Pat dough gently into a ¾-inch-thick round and cut out rounds with a 2- to 2¼-inch cutter dipped in flour. Arrange scones on prepared baking sheet. Form scraps gently into a ball. Pat out dough and cut out more scones in same manner. Brush tops of scones with reserved egg mixture and sprinkle with remaining tablespoon sugar. Bake scones in middle of oven 10 to 12 minutes, or until golden. Makes about 12 scones.

After a frosty afternoon of snow activities, you will all be ready for a nice, rejuvenating snack. Delicious Hot Rum Cider infused with cinnamon and served with Spicy Cheese Tortilla Chips can be prepared in no time. Then, while your guests are nibbling, you can cook the Mexican Bean Soup, a hot and spicy dish of tomatoes and pinto beans topped with sharp Cheddar cheese, sour cream, green chilies, and coriander. When selecting fresh chilies for the soup, look for shiny, unblemished, smooth-skinned peppers that are dry, firm, and heavy for their size. For dessert, Pecan Snowballs — shortbread rolled in confectioners' sugar — will satisfy even the most demanding sweet tooth.

Make-Ahead Information

- Pecan Snowballs keep 2 weeks in an airtight container.

A Warm-Up Snack

Hot Rum Cider

Spicy Cheese Tortilla Chips

Mexican Bean Soup

Pecan Snowballs

Vina Cumbrero Montecillo Rioja 1989

Serves 6

Hot Rum Cider

 5   cups apple cider
1/4 cup fresh lemon juice
 2   cinnamon sticks, broken in half
1/2 teaspoon salt
1 1/3 cups dark rum

Garnish: 6 lemon slices

In a saucepan bring cider and lemon juice to a simmer with cinnamon sticks and salt. Skim mixture and add rum. Heat mixture over moderate heat, stirring, until hot and divide among 6 heated mugs.

Garnish each drink with a lemon slice. Makes about 6½ cups, serving 6.

Spicy Cheese Tortilla Chips

 16 corn tortillas
     vegetable oil for brushing tortillas
1/4 teaspoon cayenne
 1   teaspoon salt
 1   teaspoon dried oregano, crumbled
1 1/2 cups coarsely grated sharp
     Cheddar cheese (about 5 ounces)

Preheat oven to 400° F.

Brush tortillas lightly with oil on one side. In a small bowl combine well cayenne, salt, and oregano and sprinkle over tortillas. Scatter Cheddar on top. Cut each tortilla into fourths with a pizza wheel or sharp knife and arrange on 3 large baking sheets. Bake tortilla wedges in 3 batches in middle of oven 10 to 12 minutes, or until golden and crisp. Serves 6.

Mexican Bean Soup

 1   large onion, chopped fine
 1   garlic clove, minced
 4   fresh hot green chilies (each about
     4 1/2 inches long), seeded and chopped
     (wear rubber gloves)
 2   tablespoons lard or vegetable oil plus
     1/4 cup vegetable oil
1 1/2 teaspoons hot chili powder
 1   1-pound can tomatoes
     including juice, chopped
 2   15-ounce cans pinto beans,
     drained and rinsed
 6   cups chicken broth
 6   corn tortillas
 2   ounces sharp Cheddar cheese,
     cut into 1/4-inch cubes

Garnish: 1/4 cup sour cream, a 3 1/2-ounce can chopped green chilies, drained, and 3 tablespoons minced fresh coriander, or to taste

In a kettle cook onion, garlic, and fresh chilies in 2 tablespoons lard or oil over moderately low heat, stirring occasionally, until vegetables are softened. Stir in chili powder and cook, stirring, 15 seconds. Add tomatoes with juice, beans, and broth and simmer 10 minutes.

While soup simmers, cut tortillas in half and stack them. Cut tortillas crosswise into ¼-inch strips. In a skillet heat remaining ¼ cup oil over moderate heat until hot but not smoking and sauté strips in batches, stirring, 15 seconds, or until crisp and pale golden, transferring as cooked to paper towels to drain. Add strips to soup and simmer 3 minutes, or until strips just begin to soften. Divide Cheddar among 6 bowls and ladle soup over it.

Garnish each serving with a dollop of sour cream, a spoonful of canned chilies, and some coriander. Makes about 9½ cups, serving 6.

Photo on page 90

Pecan Snowballs

- 1 stick (1/2 cup) unsalted butter, softened
- 1/4 teaspoon salt
- 1/4 cup confectioners' sugar plus additional for coating cookies
- 1 teaspoon vanilla
- 1/4 teaspoon almond extract
- 1 cup all-purpose flour
- 1 cup pecans, chopped fine

Preheat oven to 300° F. and lightly butter baking sheets.

In a bowl beat together butter and salt. Sift in ¼ cup sugar and beat until light and fluffy. Add vanilla, almond extract, and flour and blend well. Stir in pecans. Roll rounded teaspoons of dough into balls and bake 1 inch apart on prepared baking sheets in batches in middle of oven 20 minutes, or until golden on bottom. Transfer cookies to racks and while still warm roll in additional sugar. Cool cookies. *Cookies keep 2 weeks in an airtight container.* Makes about 40 cookies.

Saturday evening should be set aside to relax and savor the warmth of the fireside and your guests' company. Most of the dishes in this buffet can be prepared days in advance, making it virtually carefree. The spicy goat cheese *and* robust beef stew can be made weeks before. Just remember to thaw the stew in the refrigerator overnight and bring the cheese to room temperature. The gingerbread is actually enhanced if it is made a couple of days early so the flavors of the spices, molasses, and coffee can meld together. All that is left is a pea, lettuce, and onion side dish that can be made in a snap!

Make-Ahead Information

- Lemon-Thyme-Marinated Goat Cheese *must* be marinated, covered and chilled, at least 1 week and up to 3 weeks.

- Beef Stew with Olives and Rum may be prepared, in part, 2 days ahead and chilled, covered, or kept frozen 2 weeks.

- Prune Armagnac Gingerbread may be made 2 days ahead and kept covered at room temperature.

Buffet Dinner by the Fire

Lemon-Thyme-Marinated Goat Cheese

Beef Stew with Olives and Rum

Peas with Lettuce and Onions

Crusty Bread (store-bought)

Prune Armagnac Gingerbread

Produttori del Barbaresco
Barbaresco 1989

Serves 6

Lemon-Thyme-Marinated Goat Cheese

1   12-ounce log of mild goat cheese, cut crosswise into 4 pieces
1/2   lemon, sliced thin
3   large shallots, sliced thin
6 to 8   fresh thyme sprigs
1   teaspoon dried hot red pepper flakes
about 1 1/2 cups olive oil

In a 1-quart glass jar with a tight-fitting lid combine goat cheese, lemon, shallots, thyme, and red pepper flakes and add enough oil to jar to cover cheese completely. *Marinate cheese, covered and chilled, at least 1 week and up to 3 weeks.* Let cheese come to room temperature before serving. Serves 6.

Beef Stew with Olives and Rum

3   bacon slices, chopped
2 1/2   pounds boneless lean chuck, cut into 1-inch pieces
1   tablespoon olive oil
1   large onion, chopped
3   garlic cloves, minced
1   32-ounce can whole tomatoes including juice
1/3   cup dark rum
3   3-inch strips orange zest removed with vegetable peeler
3   large fresh parsley sprigs
1   bay leaf
1/8   teaspoon dried thyme, crumbled
1   cup small pimiento-stuffed olives

Garnish: 1 tablespoon minced fresh parsley leaves
Accompaniment: cooked noodles or steamed rice (page 169)

In a large kettle cook bacon over moderate heat, stirring, until crisp and with a slotted spoon transfer to a bowl. In drippings remaining in kettle brown beef in batches, transferring as browned to bowl.

Preheat oven to 300° F.

Add oil to drippings in kettle and cook onion and garlic over moderate heat until softened. Add tomatoes with juice, rum, zest, parsley sprigs, bay leaf, and thyme, stirring to break up tomatoes. Add beef and bacon and bring to a boil. Braise stew, covered, in oven 1 hour, or until beef is tender when pierced with a fork. Discard zest and bay leaf. *Stew may be prepared up to this point and cooled completely before chilling, covered, 2 days or kept frozen 2 weeks. Reheat stew (thawed if necessary) over moderate heat, stirring, before proceeding with recipe.* Stir olives into stew. If necessary, cook stew, uncovered, over moderate heat, stirring occasionally, until liquid is reduced to a sauce-like consistency.

Serve stew, garnished with minced parsley, with noodles or rice. Serves 6 generously.

Peas with Lettuce and Onions

1 1/2   cups sliced small white onions
1/2   stick (1/4 cup) unsalted butter
1   large head romaine (about 1 3/4 pounds), cut into julienne strips
3   pounds fresh peas, shelled (about 3 cups)
a cheesecloth bag containing 1 tablespoon fresh thyme or 1 teaspoon dried, 1 bay leaf, and 1/2 teaspoon dried mint
1/2   teaspoon sugar
1/2   cup water
1/4   cup minced fresh mint leaves, or to taste

In a large saucepan cook onions in butter over moderate heat, stirring, until softened. Add romaine, peas, cheesecloth bag, sugar, and salt and pepper to taste and cook, stirring, 3 minutes. Add water and simmer, covered, until peas are just tender, 8 to 10 minutes. Stir in fresh mint and salt and pepper to taste and discard cheesecloth bag. Serves 6.

Prune Armagnac Gingerbread

      unsweetened cocoa powder for dusting pan
  1   cup chopped pitted prunes
1/2   cup Armagnac or Cognac
  1   tablespoon minced fresh peeled gingerroot
  3   cups all-purpose flour
  2   teaspoons baking soda
  2   teaspoons cinnamon
  1   teaspoon ground ginger
  1   teaspoon ground cloves
1/8   teaspoon cayenne
3/4   teaspoon salt
  1   cup vegetable shortening at room temperature
1 1/2 cups firmly packed light brown sugar
  1   cup unsulfured molasses
1/2   cup strong brewed coffee
  4   large eggs, beaten lightly
  1   teaspoon vanilla
1/2   cup chopped crystallized ginger

Garnish: sliced kumquats
*Accompaniment: crème fraîche
or sour cream*

Preheat oven to 350° F. Butter a 10-inch spring-form pan and dust with cocoa powder, knocking out excess.

In a skillet cook prunes, Armagnac or Cognac, and gingerroot over moderately high heat, stirring frequently, until almost all liquid is evaporated and remove skillet from heat.

Into a bowl sift flour, baking soda, spices, and salt. In a large bowl with an electric mixer cream shortening. Add sugar, beating until light and fluffy. Add molasses in a stream, beating until combined well. Add flour mixture, coffee, eggs, and vanilla, beating until just combined. (Batter may separate at this point.) Reserve 1 tablespoon crystallized ginger and stir remainder into batter with prune mixture.

Turn batter into prepared pan and sprinkle with reserved ginger. Bake gingerbread in oven 1 hour 20 minutes, or until a tester comes out clean, and cool on a rack 1 hour. (Gingerbread will fall slightly in center.) *Gingerbread may be made 2 days ahead and kept covered at room temperature.*

Garnish gingerbread with kumquats and serve warm or at room temperature with *crème fraîche* or sour cream.

Photo on page 94

Whether your guests choose to sleep in or take a few more runs on the slopes, you will want to give them a nourishing lunch before they head home. Our quick *fusilli* dish celebrates the hearty flavor of collards. Nutritious and high in fiber, collard leaves should be young and green and have a velvety feel. To accompany the pasta, we suggest a tangy mixed green salad with grapefruit. Look for smooth, slick, thin-skinned grapefruits that are heavy and firm. No refrigeration is required if they are used within a week. And, finally, the chocolate-dipped shortbread wedges are a wonderful treat; any leftovers can be packed up easily for your guests to enjoy in the car.

Make-Ahead Information

- Dressing for Mixed Greens with Grapefruit, Fennel, and Parmesan may be prepared, in part, 1 day ahead and chilled, covered.

- Shortbread for Chocolate-Dipped Hazelnut Shortbread Wedges may be made 2 days ahead and kept in an airtight container.

A Quick Farewell Lunch

Fusilli with Collards, Bacon, and Garlic

Mixed Greens with Grapefruit, Fennel, and Parmesan

Chocolate-Dipped Hazelnut Shortbread Wedges

Nalle Dry Creek Valley Zinfandel 1992

Serves 6

Fusilli with Collards, Bacon, and Garlic

1 1/2   pounds collards, coarse stems discarded and leaves washed well and chopped coarse

6   ounces sliced bacon, cut into 1/2-inch pieces

6   large garlic cloves, chopped fine

2   onions, sliced thin

1/4   teaspoon dried hot red pepper flakes, or to taste

1/3   cup olive oil

1 1/4   pounds *fusilli* (spiral-shaped pasta)

1 1/2   tablespoons red-wine vinegar

Accompaniment: **freshly grated Parmesan cheese**

In a large kettle of boiling water cook collards 10 minutes. Drain collards in a colander set over a large bowl and return cooking liquid to kettle. In a large skillet cook bacon over moderate heat, stirring, until just browned and transfer with a slotted spoon to a small bowl. Pour off fat from skillet and in skillet cook garlic, onions, and red pepper flakes in half of oil over moderately low heat, stirring, until onion is softened and garlic is golden brown.

Bring cooking liquid to a boil and in it cook *fusilli* until *al dente*. Drain *fusilli* well. To onion mixture add collards, bacon, *fusilli*, remaining oil, and vinegar and toss well with salt and pepper to taste.

Serve pasta sprinkled with Parmesan. Serves 6.

Photo on page 98

Mixed Greens with Grapefruit, Fennel, and Parmesan

For dressing

1   small garlic clove, minced and mashed to a paste with 1/4 teaspoon salt

3   tablespoons fresh grapefruit juice

3   tablespoons white-wine vinegar

1 1/2   teaspoons Dijon mustard

1/2   cup olive oil

1/3   cup minced fresh parsley leaves (preferably flat-leafed)

8   cups coarsely shredded romaine

3   cups *arugula* or watercress, coarse stems discarded and leaves washed well and spun dry

3   cups thinly sliced fennel (sometimes called anise)

1   cup thinly sliced radishes

3   ounces Parmesan cheese, shaved into curls with a vegetable peeler (about 1 1/2 cups)

3   large grapefruit, zest and pith cut away with a serrated knife and fruit cut into sections

Make dressing:

In a small bowl whisk together garlic paste, grapefruit juice, vinegar, and mustard. Add oil in a stream, whisking until emulsified. *Dressing may be prepared up to this point 1 day ahead and chilled, covered.* Whisk in parsley and salt and pepper to taste.

In a large bowl toss together romaine, *arugula* or watercress, fennel, radishes, and dressing. Add Parmesan and grapefruit sections, cut into 1-inch pieces, and toss gently. Serves 6.

Photo on page 158

Chocolate-Dipped Hazelnut Shortbread Wedges

1 1/4	cups hazelnuts with skins (about 6 ounces), toasted
1 1/4	cups all-purpose flour
1/2	cup plus 2 tablespoons sugar
1 1/4	sticks (10 tablespoons) unsalted butter, melted and cooled
4	ounces fine-quality bittersweet or semisweet chocolate (not unsweetened)
1	tablespoon vegetable shortening

Preheat oven to 350° F. and butter and flour two 8-inch round cake pans.

In a food processor grind hazelnuts fine with flour and sugar. Add butter and blend until combined well. Press half of dough evenly onto bottom of each pan. Cut through each round of dough with a small knife to score 16 wedges and bake in middle of oven 20 minutes, or until pale golden. While shortbread is still warm, score rounds again and cool in pans on a rack. Choose 2 plates slightly smaller than pans. Put a plate directly on surface of each shortbread and invert shortbread carefully onto it. *Shortbread may be made 2 days ahead and kept in an airtight container.*

In a metal bowl set over a saucepan of simmering water melt chocolate with shortening, stirring until smooth, and transfer to a deep narrow cup or glass measure. Dip points of shortbread wedges into chocolate, coating them halfway and letting any excess drip off. Transfer shortbread wedges as dipped to a rack set over a sheet of wax paper and let stand until chocolate is set. Makes 32 cookies.

more breakfast & brunch dishes

Cornmeal Porridge with Dried Fruit (page 104)

Cornmeal Porridge with Dried Fruit

1/2 cup golden raisins
1 1/2 cups yellow cornmeal
1 cup cold water plus 2 3/4 cups boiling water
3/4 teaspoon salt, or to taste
1 cup milk
3 tablespoons unsalted butter, cut into bits
24 dried apricots, cut into pieces

Accompaniments
light brown sugar or maple syrup
milk

In a small bowl soak raisins in enough cold water to cover 10 minutes and drain well. In a saucepan whisk together cornmeal, cold water, and salt until smooth and add milk and boiling water in a slow stream, whisking. Cook mixture in top of a double boiler set over simmering water, stirring frequently, 10 to 15 minutes, or until liquid is absorbed and porridge is thickened.

Divide porridge among 6 bowls and top with butter, apricots, and raisins. Serve porridge with sugar or syrup and milk. Serves 6.

Photo on page 102

Mixed Berry French Toast Pudding

4 cups mixed berries such as blueberries, raspberries, or blackberries, picked-over
1 cup plus 1 tablespoon sugar
1 teaspoon cinnamon
2 large eggs, beaten lightly
1/2 cup milk
1 teaspoon vanilla
10 slices French bread (cut on the diagonal 1/2 inch thick)

Accompaniment: lightly sweetened sour cream

Preheat oven to 400° F.

In a shallow 2-quart casserole sprinkle berries with 1 cup sugar and cinnamon. In a bowl combine eggs, milk, and vanilla. Add bread and soak, turning, 3 to 5 minutes, or until saturated. Arrange bread in one layer over berries and sprinkle with remaining tablespoon sugar. Bake pudding in middle of oven 20 to 25 minutes, or until bread is golden brown.

Serve French toast topped with berry sauce and a dollop of sour cream. Serves 6.

Banana Buttermilk Griddlecakes

2 1/4   cups all-purpose flour
3 1/4   teaspoons baking powder
1 1/8   teaspoons cinnamon
  3/4   teaspoon baking soda
  1/2   teaspoon salt
    4   large egg yolks and 5 large egg whites
    6   tablespoons sugar
2 1/4   cups buttermilk
    3   tablespoons unsalted butter, melted
        and cooled, plus additional melted
        butter for brushing griddle and griddlecakes
    1   tablespoon freshly grated lemon zest
1 1/2   teaspoons vanilla
    3   cups coarsely chopped banana
        (about 5 bananas)
        a pinch cream of tartar

Accompaniment: warm maple syrup

In a bowl whisk together flour, baking powder,
cinnamon, baking soda, and salt. In a large bowl
beat yolks with sugar until mixture is light. Beat in
buttermilk, 3 tablespoons butter, zest, and vanilla
and stir in banana. Stir flour mixture into egg
mixture until just combined. In another bowl beat
whites with cream of tartar and a pinch salt until
they hold stiff peaks and fold into batter.

Preheat oven to 200° F.

Heat a heavy griddle over moderately
high heat until hot and brush with additional
melted butter. Using a ¼-cup measure pour batter
onto griddle and cook 1½ to 2 minutes on each
side, or until golden brown, transferring as
cooked to a heatproof platter. Brush griddlecakes
with additional butter and keep warm, covered,
in oven.

Serve griddlecakes with maple syrup.
Makes about 30 griddlecakes, serving 6.

Smoked Salmon Spread

12   ounces cream cheese, softened
 3   tablespoons sour cream
 1   tablespoon fresh lemon juice
1/3 cup minced scallion or sweet onion
 1   tablespoon minced fresh dill
1/2 pound smoked salmon or lox, chopped
 3   tablespoons drained bottled capers

Accompaniment: 6 bagels or bialys,
halved and toasted

In a bowl with an electric mixer beat cream
cheese and sour cream until light and fluffy. Beat
in lemon juice, scallion or onion, dill, and pepper
to taste until combined well. Stir in salmon or lox
and capers and transfer to a crock. *Spread may be
made 2 days ahead and chilled, covered.*

Serve spread with bagels or bialys. Makes
about 3 cups, serving 6.

Prune and Pecan Caramel Sticky Buns

1   1/4-ounce package active dry yeast
     (2 1/2 teaspoons)
1/4 cup granulated sugar
6   tablespoons lukewarm water
2 1/2 cups all-purpose flour plus
     additional for sprinkling dough
1   teaspoon salt
1/4 cup milk
1   teaspoon vanilla
2   large eggs
1/2 stick (1/4 cup) unsalted butter,
     cut into pieces and softened
     For caramel
3/4 cup firmly packed light brown sugar
3/4 stick (6 tablespoons)
     unsalted butter, melted
2   tablespoons dark corn syrup
     For filling
3/4 cup pecans, chopped fine
1 1/2 cups prune purée (recipe follows)

In a small bowl proof yeast with ¼ teaspoon sugar in lukewarm water 5 to 10 minutes, or until foamy. In a standing electric mixer fitted with paddle attachment beat together yeast mixture, remaining sugar, 2½ cups flour, salt, milk, vanilla, and eggs at low speed until combined well. Beat in butter, a few pieces at a time, and beat at medium speed 5 to 7 minutes, or until smooth and elastic. (Dough will be very sticky.) Scrape dough from side of bowl and sprinkle lightly with additional flour. Let dough rise, covered with plastic wrap and a kitchen towel, in a warm place 1 hour, or until doubled in bulk.

Make caramel while dough is rising:
Butter a 13- by 9-inch baking pan.

In a bowl whisk together caramel ingredients until combined well and pour into prepared pan, spreading evenly.

Make filling while dough is rising:
In a bowl combine well pecans and prune purée.

Punch down dough and on a well-floured surface pat or roll it into a 16- by 12-inch rectangle. Spread filling on dough, leaving a ½-inch border on long sides. With a long side facing you, roll up dough jelly-roll fashion, brushing off any excess flour, and pinch edges together firmly to seal. Cut dough crosswise into 12 pieces with a sharp knife and arrange pieces, cut sides down, on caramel in pan. Let buns rise, covered loosely, in a warm place 45 to 50 minutes, or until doubled in bulk.

Preheat oven to 350° F.

Bake buns in middle of oven 30 to 35 minutes, or until golden. Invert buns carefully onto a large heatproof platter and cool slightly.

Serve sticky buns warm. Makes 12 buns.

Photo opposite

⊙ Prune Purée

3   cups pitted prunes (about 1 1/2 pounds)
1 1/2 cups fresh orange juice
1/2 cup sugar

In a saucepan combine all ingredients and cook, covered, over moderately low heat, stirring occasionally, 20 to 25 minutes, or until prunes are tender and cooking liquid is syrupy. Cool mixture and purée in a food processor. Makes about 3 cups.

Brandied Apricot Almond Bread

    1   cup chopped dried apricots
        (about 6 ounces)
    2   tablespoons brandy
    3   cups all-purpose flour
1 1/4   teaspoons salt
    1   teaspoon baking soda
    2   teaspoons baking powder
    1   cup chopped almonds (about 5 ounces),
        toasted and cooled
  1/4   cup vegetable shortening at
        room temperature
    1   cup sugar
    2   large eggs, beaten lightly
    1   cup buttermilk
  1/2   teaspoon almond extract

In a small bowl soak dried apricots in brandy 30 minutes, or until brandy is absorbed.

Preheat oven to 350° F. and grease a loaf pan, 9¼ by 5¼ by 2¾ inches.

In a bowl stir together flour, salt, baking soda, baking powder, and almonds. In a large bowl stir together shortening and sugar and add eggs, combining well. Stir in buttermilk and almond extract, combining well. Add flour mixture and stir until just combined. Stir in apricot mixture and spoon into prepared pan.

Bake bread in middle of oven 1 hour to 1 hour and 10 minutes, or until a tester comes out clean. Cool bread in pan on a rack 10 minutes. Loosen edge with a knife and turn bread right side up onto rack. Cool bread completely. *Bread keeps, wrapped tightly in foil and chilled, 5 days or, frozen, 2 weeks.*

Serve bread, sliced, at room temperature or toasted. Makes 1 loaf.

Blueberry Pecan Crumb Cake

1 3/4   cups all-purpose flour
    1   teaspoon baking powder
    1   teaspoon baking soda
  1/4   teaspoon salt
  1/2   stick (1/4 cup) unsalted butter, softened
  1/4   cup vegetable shortening at
        room temperature
    1   cup granulated sugar
    3   large eggs, beaten lightly
    1   cup sour cream
    3   teaspoons freshly grated lemon zest
    3   cups blueberries, picked-over and tossed with
        1 tablespoon flour
        For topping
    1   cup firmly packed light brown sugar
  1/4   cup all-purpose flour
  1/2   cup finely chopped pecans
  1/2   stick (1/4 cup) cold unsalted butter,
        cut into bits

Preheat oven to 350° F. Butter and flour a 13- by 9-inch baking pan, knocking out excess.

In a bowl stir together flour, baking powder, baking soda, and salt. In a large bowl cream together butter, shortening, and sugar until light and fluffy. Beat in eggs, 1 at a time, beating well after each addition, and add sour cream alternately in batches with flour mixture, stirring until just combined. Fold in zest and blueberries and spread in prepared baking pan.

Make topping:

In a small bowl stir together sugar, flour, and pecans and blend in butter until mixture resembles coarse meal.

Sprinkle topping evenly over batter and bake in middle of oven 50 minutes, or until a tester inserted in center comes out clean. Cool cake in pan on a rack 10 minutes.

Serve cake cut into squares.

Cinnamon Raisin Cream Scones

- 1/2 cup heavy cream plus additional for brushing scones
- 1 large egg
- 1 teaspoon vanilla
- 3 tablespoons firmly packed light brown sugar
- 2 1/3 cups cake flour (not self-rising)
- 1 teaspoon cinnamon
- 1/2 teaspoon salt
- 1 tablespoon baking powder
- 1/2 teaspoon baking soda
- 3/4 stick (6 tablespoons) cold unsalted butter, cut into bits
- 1/2 cup raisins
  granulated sugar for sprinkling scones

Preheat oven to 400° F.

In a bowl whisk together ½ cup cream, egg, vanilla, and brown sugar until combined well. In another bowl stir together flour, cinnamon, salt, baking powder, and baking soda and blend in butter until mixture resembles coarse meal. Stir in raisins and cream mixture with a fork until mixture just forms a sticky but manageable dough. On a lightly floured surface knead dough gently 30 seconds. Pat dough into a ¾-inch-thick round and cut into 6 wedges. On an ungreased baking sheet brush scones with additional cream and sprinkle with granulated sugar. Bake scones in middle of oven 15 to 18 minutes, or until golden. Makes 6 large scones.

Spiced Winter Fruit Compote

- 1 cup firmly packed light brown sugar
- 1 1/2 cups water
- 3 cinnamon sticks
- 6 whole allspice
- 3/4 teaspoon anise seeds
- 4 pears, peeled, cored, and cut into eighths
- 1/2 cup raisins
- 4 large navel oranges, peel and pith discarded and fruit cut crosswise into 1/2-inch-thick slices
- 2 grapefruits, peel and pith discarded and fruit cut into sections

In a stainless-steel or enameled kettle combine sugar, water, and spices and bring to a boil, stirring. Boil mixture 5 minutes. Add pears and raisins and simmer, stirring occasionally, 15 to 20 minutes, or until pears are just tender. While pears and raisins are cooking, in a heatproof shallow dish combine oranges and grapefruit. Transfer pears and raisins with a slotted spoon to heatproof dish and combine with oranges and grapefruit. Boil syrup until reduced by half and pour through a sieve onto fruit. Stir fruit gently to combine and let cool. Chill compote, uncovered, 1 hour. Serves 6.

Blueberry and Melon Salad with Yogurt Mint Dressing

2 tablespoons blueberry vinegar
   (recipe follows) or fresh lemon juice
3 tablespoons vegetable oil
1/2 cup plain yogurt
2 tablespoons half-and-half
2 teaspoons honey, or to taste
1 tablespoon minced fresh mint leaves
1 honeydew melon, scooped into balls
   with a 1-inch melon-ball cutter
1 cantaloupe, scooped into balls with
   a 1-inch melon-ball cutter
2 cups blueberries, picked over

Garnish: fresh mint leaves

In a small bowl whisk together blueberry vinegar or lemon juice and oil until emulsified. Whisk in yogurt, half-and-half, honey, and mint and chill, covered, 30 minutes. In a large serving bowl combine melon balls and blueberries.

Garnish salad with mint leaves and serve with dressing. Serves 6.

Blueberry Vinegar

3 cups blueberries, picked over
2 cups distilled white vinegar

Rinse a heatproof 1½-quart jar with a non metalic lid with boiling water and drain. Put blueberries in jar. In a stainless-steel or enameled saucepan bring vinegar just to a boil. Pour vinegar into jar and seal tightly with lid. Let vinegar stand in a cool, dark place 3 weeks.

Strain vinegar through a very fine sieve lined with a triple thickness of rinsed and squeezed cheesecloth into a stainless-steel or enameled saucepan. Bring vinegar to a boil and pour into a sterilized bottle (procedure follows), sealing with lid. Store vinegar in a cool, dark place. Makes about 3 cups.

To Sterilize Bottles

Wash bottles in hot suds and rinse in scalding water. Put bottles in a kettle and cover with hot water. Bring water to a boil, covered, and boil bottles 15 minutes from time that steam emerges from kettle. Turn off heat and let bottles stand in hot water. Just before filling invert bottles onto a kitchen towel to dry. Bottles should be filled while still hot. Sterilize bottle lids 5 minutes, or according to manufacturer's instructions.

Baked Eggs with Sausage, Peppers, and Potatoes

1	pound boiling potatoes
3	tablespoons olive oil
1	tablespoon unsalted butter
1	pound *chorizo** (spicy pork sausage), pricked lightly with a needle
4	cups thinly sliced onion
2	green peppers, sliced thin
4	garlic cloves, minced
1	1-pound can whole tomatoes, drained and chopped
1/2	cup dry red wine
3	tablespoons red-wine vinegar, or to taste
2	teaspoons dried oregano, crumbled
2	teaspoons dried basil, crumbled
	cayenne to taste
6	large eggs

Garnish: minced fresh parsley leaves

*available at Hispanic markets and many supermarkets

In a saucepan combine potatoes with cold water to cover and bring to a boil. Simmer potatoes, covered, 25 to 30 minutes, or until just tender. Drain potatoes and peel. Chill potatoes, loosely covered, 1 hour.

Dice potatoes and in a skillet sauté in 1 tablespoon oil and butter over moderately high heat 5 minutes, or until golden.

In a large stainless-steel or enameled skillet sauté *chorizo* in remaining 2 tablespoons oil over moderately high heat 5 minutes, or until golden brown, and transfer with a slotted spoon to a cutting board to cool. Pour off all but 2 tablespoons fat from skillet.

Preheat oven to 350° F.

Add onion to skillet and cook over moderate heat, stirring, until softened. Add peppers and garlic and cook, stirring occasionally, until onion is golden. Cut *chorizo* into ½-inch-thick slices. Add *chorizo* and tomatoes to skillet and cook, stirring, 2 minutes. Add wine, vinegar, oregano, basil, cayenne, and salt and pepper to taste and cook, stirring, 10 minutes, or until excess liquid is evaporated but mixture is still moist. Stir in potatoes gently and transfer mixture to a 1½-quart gratin dish (11 by 8 by 2 inches), spreading evenly. *Potato and* chorizo *mixture may be made 1 day ahead and chilled, covered.* Bake mixture in oven 10 to 20 minutes, or until hot. Make 6 depressions in mixture with a ladle or a large spoon. Break 1 egg carefully into each depression and bake an additional 15 to 20 minutes, or until eggs are set.

Garnish dish with parsley. Serves 6.

Deviled Ham and Eggs

10	hard-cooked large eggs
1/2	cup finely chopped cooked ham
1/4	cup Dijon mustard
1/4	cup mayonnaise
1	teaspoon white-wine vinegar
1/4	teaspoon Tabasco
3	tablespoons minced onion
1	tablespoon minced sweet pickle
2	to 3 tablespoons water

Halve eggs lengthwise and force yolks through a sieve into a bowl. Stir in remaining ingredients, adding enough water to reach desired consistency and salt and pepper to taste. Mound filling in whites. Makes 20 deviled egg halves.

Scrambled Egg Burritos

12 large eggs
 3 tablespoons minced fresh coriander
1/2 cup minced scallion including greens
1/4 cup milk
 3 tablespoons unsalted butter
 2 cups coarsely grated Monterey Jack cheese
12 warm 7-inch flour tortillas

Accompaniment: tomato *salsa* (page 198) or store-bought

In a bowl whisk together eggs, coriander, scallion, milk, and salt and pepper to taste. In a large heavy saucepan melt butter over moderate heat until foamy. Add egg mixture and reduce heat to moderately low. Cook egg mixture, stirring, 3 to 5 minutes, or until just set. Divide egg mixture and Monterey Jack among tortillas and roll tortillas, enclosing filling.

Serve *burritos* with *salsa*. Serves 6.

Tarragon Scrambled Eggs in Tulip Croustades

18 slices soft white bread, crusts discarded
    vegetable oil for brushing bread
12 large eggs
1/3 cup minced fresh tarragon or 1 tablespoon dried, crumbled
3/4 cup minced scallion including greens
1/3 cup milk
1/2 stick (1/4 cup) unsalted butter

Garnish: tarragon sprigs

Preheat oven to 350° F.

Roll each slice of bread flat with a rolling pin and brush both sides of each slice with some oil. Fit each slice gently into a ½-cup muffin tin and bake in oven 20 minutes, or until edges are golden. Croustades *may be made 1 day ahead and kept in an airtight container at room temperature. Reheat croustades, if necessary, in a preheated 300° F. oven 10 minutes.*

In a bowl whisk together eggs, tarragon, scallion, milk, and salt and pepper to taste. In a large heavy saucepan melt butter over moderate heat until foamy. Add egg mixture and reduce heat to moderately low. Cook egg mixture, stirring with a whisk, 3 to 5 minutes, or until just set. (Scrambled eggs should have small curds and appear very creamy.)

Divide eggs among *croustades* and garnish with tarragon sprigs. Serves 6.

Photo opposite

Tarragon Scrambled Eggs in Tulip Croustades

Chicken Nachos

      3 cups chicken broth
      1 whole boneless skinless chicken
         breast, halved
      2 scallions, minced
    1/4 cup minced red bell pepper
      1 tablespoon vegetable oil
  1 1/4 cups chopped seeded vine-ripened cherry
         tomatoes
      2 tablespoons minced fresh coriander,
         or to taste
      1 tablespoon minced pickled *jalapeño*
         chilies, or to taste
         about 40 corn tortilla chips
    1/2 pound sliced Monterey Jack cheese,
         cut into triangles the size of tortilla chips

In a skillet bring chicken broth to a boil and in it cook chicken at a bare simmer, turning once, 7 minutes. Remove skillet from heat and cool chicken in broth. Transfer chicken to a cutting board and shred with a fork. Reserve broth for another use.

Preheat oven to 425° F.

In another skillet cook scallions and bell pepper in oil over moderately low heat, stirring, until scallions are softened. Stir in tomatoes, coriander, *jalapeños*, and chicken and cook until just heated through. Divide mixture among tortilla chips. Arrange chips in one layer in shallow baking pans and top with Monterey Jack. Bake *nachos* in oven 5 minutes, or until cheese is melted. Makes about 40 *nachos*.

Onion, Bacon, and Cream Kuchen

         For dough
      5 teaspoons active dry yeast
         (two 1/4-ounce packages)
      1 cup lukewarm milk
  3 1/2 to 4 cups all-purpose flour
      1 teaspoon sugar
      2 large eggs, beaten lightly
    1/2 stick (1/4 cup) unsalted butter, softened
      2 teaspoons salt

    1/2 pound sliced bacon, cut into 1-inch pieces
    3/4 stick (6 tablespoons) unsalted butter
      2 pounds onions, sliced thin
    1/2 cup dry white wine
      1 cup heavy cream
      1 teaspoon Dijon mustard, or to taste
         freshly grated nutmeg to taste

Make dough:

In a large bowl proof yeast in ½ cup lukewarm milk with 1 tablespoon flour and sugar 15 minutes, or until foamy. Add remaining ½ cup milk and eggs and combine well. Stir in 3½ cups flour, butter, and salt. In a standing electric mixer fitted with dough hook beat dough, adding more flour if necessary, 5 minutes, or until smooth and elastic. (Alternately, knead dough on a floured surface, adding more flour if necessary, 10 minutes, or until smooth and elastic.) Put dough in a buttered bowl and turn to coat with butter. Let dough rise, covered tightly with plastic wrap, in a warm place 1 hour, or until doubled in bulk. *(Alternately, let dough rise, covered and chilled, overnight. Let dough come to room temperature before rolling out.)*

In a large skillet cook bacon over moderate heat, stirring, until golden brown and transfer to paper towels to drain. Pour off all but 3 tablespoons fat from skillet and add 3 tablespoons butter, onions, and salt and pepper to taste. Cook mixture, stirring occasionally, until onions are golden. Add wine and reduce liquid over moderately high heat, stirring, 1 minute. Add cream and reduce liquid, stirring, until thick. Stir in mustard, nutmeg, salt and pepper to taste, and bacon and cool. *Onion mixture may be prepared 1 day ahead and chilled, covered.*

Preheat oven to 550° F. Butter and flour a shallow baking pan, knocking out excess.

Roll dough into a 17- by 12-inch rectangle and transfer to prepared pan. Prick dough lightly with a fork. Spread onion mixture on dough, leaving a 1-inch border on all sides, and dot top with remaining 3 tablespoons butter. Bake kuchen in middle of oven 10 minutes, or until top is golden brown and bubbling. Serves 6.

Ham and Cheddar Pudding

1	onion, minced
1	stick (1/2 cup) unsalted butter, softened
1 1/2	pounds cooked smoked ham, cut into 1-inch cubes
10	slices homemade-type white bread
2	canned mild green chilies, seeded and minced
1/2	pound sharp Cheddar cheese, grated
3	cups milk
4	large eggs, beaten lightly
2	teaspoons Dijon mustard, or to taste
1/4	teaspoon cayenne

In a large skillet cook onion in 2 tablespoons butter over moderate heat, stirring, until softened and add ham. Cook mixture, stirring occasionally, 5 minutes and cool. Spread remaining 6 tablespoons butter on bread and cut into 1-inch cubes.

In prepared baking dish spread half of bread cubes and top with half of ham. Top ham with half of chilies and half of Cheddar. Layer remaining bread cubes, ham, chilies, and Cheddar in same manner.

In a bowl whisk together milk, eggs, mustard, cayenne, and salt and pepper to taste until combined well and pour over Cheddar. *Chill mixture, covered, at least 3 hours or overnight.*

Preheat oven to 350° F. and butter a large baking dish.

Let mixture come to room temperature and bake in dish, covered with foil, set in a baking pan of hot water in middle of oven 45 minutes. Bake pudding, uncovered, 45 minutes more, or until puffed and golden. Serves 6 to 8.

Tomato, Sausage, and Cheese Tart

1   recipe pastry dough (page 23)
    raw rice for weighting shell
1/2 pound Italian sausage, casings discarded
1   cup sliced scallion
2   tablespoons Dijon mustard
1   cup grated mozzarella cheese
2   pounds vine-ripened tomatoes, peeled, cored, and cut into 1/3-inch-thick slices
1   large egg
1/2 cup heavy cream
    dried oregano, crumbled, to taste

On a floured surface roll out dough ⅛ inch thick into a round and fit into a 9¼-inch flan or tart pan with a removable fluted ring. Roll a floured rolling pin over rim to trim edge and prick bottom of shell with a fork. Chill shell 1 hour.

Preheat oven to 425° F.

Line shell with wax paper and fill paper with raw rice. Bake shell in lower third of oven 10 to 15 minutes, or until it begins to set. Remove rice and paper carefully and bake shell 10 to 15 minutes more, or until golden. Cool shell in pan on a rack. *Shell may be made 1 day ahead and chilled, covered.*

In a skillet cook sausage over moderate heat, stirring, 7 to 10 minutes, or until no longer pink. Add scallion and cook 5 minutes. Drain sausage mixture in a sieve 15 minutes. *Sausage mixture may be made 1 day ahead and chilled, covered.*

Brush bottom of shell with mustard and sprinkle with ½ cup mozzarella. Spoon sausage mixture evenly over mozzarella and top with tomatoes, overlapping in concentric circles. In a bowl beat egg lightly with cream and spoon over tomatoes. Sprinkle custard with oregano, salt and pepper to taste, and remaining ½ cup mozzarella. Bake tart in middle of oven 20 minutes and cool in pan on a rack 10 minutes. Serves 6 to 8.

Tomato and Onion Sandwiches

For basil mayonnaise
1   cup mayonnaise
1   tablespoon fresh lemon juice
2   cups packed fresh basil leaves, minced

3   large vine-ripened tomatoes, peeled, seeded, and cut into 1/4-inch-thick slices
12 slices homemade-type white bread
1   large red onion, sliced as thin as possible and separated into rings

Make basil mayonnaise:

In a bowl stir together mayonnaise, lemon juice, and basil. *Basil mayonnaise may be made 1 day ahead and chilled, covered.*

Sprinkle both sides of tomato slices with salt and let stand on a rack 30 minutes.

Trim crusts from bread and spread 1 side of each slice with a thin layer of basil mayonnaise. Divide half of onion among 6 bread slices. Top onion with tomato slices, remaining onion, and remaining bread slices, pressing sandwiches together gently.

Cut sandwiches diagonally into quarters. Serves 6.

Corn Chowder with Ham and Scallions

1/2 pound ham steak, cut into 1/4-inch dice
2   tablespoons unsalted butter
1   large onion, chopped
1   cup chopped celery
3   large boiling potatoes (about 1 1/2 pounds)
4   cups water
2   cups fresh corn or a 10-ounce package frozen, thawed
2   cups milk
1 1/2 cups half-and-half
1/4 teaspoon dried thyme, crumbled
2/3 cup sliced scallion
    Tabasco to taste

In a kettle cook ham over moderately low heat, stirring, until it begins to brown. Add butter, onion, and celery and cook, stirring, until onion is softened. Peel potatoes and cut into ½-inch cubes. Add potatoes and water to onion mixture and bring to a boil. Simmer potatoes, covered, 10 minutes, or until barely tender. Add corn, milk, half-and-half, thyme, and pepper to taste. Bring liquid to a boil and simmer, uncovered, 15 minutes, or until potatoes are tender. *Chowder may be made up to this point 2 days ahead, cooled completely, and chilled, covered.* Stir in scallion, Tabasco, and salt and pepper to taste. Makes about 14 cups, serving 6 to 8.

☺+ Bloody Mary Gazpacho

3	pounds vine-ripened tomatoes, quartered
3/4	cup tomato juice
2	teaspoons drained bottled horseradish
1/2	teaspoon sugar
1	cup finely chopped peeled seeded cucumber
1/2	cup finely chopped sweet onion
1/2	cup finely chopped yellow bell pepper
1/2	cup finely chopped celery
2	tablespoons vodka if desired
1/4	teaspoon Tabasco, or to taste
1	tablespoon Worcestershire sauce

In a blender blend tomatoes, tomato juice, horseradish, and sugar until smooth and strain through a sieve into a bowl. Stir in remaining ingredients and enough water to thin soup to desired consistency and season with salt and pepper to taste. *Chill* gazpacho, *covered, at least 1 hour, or until cold, and up to 1 day ahead.* Makes about 7 cups, serving 6.

Mustard Buttermilk Yeast Biscuits

2	tablespoons active dry yeast
1	tablespoon honey
2	tablespoons lukewarm water
2 1/2	cups sifted cake flour (not self-rising)
1 1/2	teaspoons salt
1/2	teaspoon freshly ground black pepper
1	teaspoon baking powder
1/2	teaspoon baking soda
3	tablespoons cold unsalted butter, cut into bits, plus melted butter for brushing biscuits
2/3	cup buttermilk
1/4	cup coarse-grained mustard

Butter a baking pan.

In a small bowl proof yeast with honey in lukewarm water 15 minutes, or until foamy. Into a bowl sift together flour, salt, pepper, baking powder, and baking soda. Add 3 tablespoons butter and blend until mixture resembles meal. Add buttermilk, mustard, and yeast mixture and stir until just combined. On a floured surface knead dough very lightly until it just holds together. Pat out dough ½ inch thick into a rectangle and with a 2-inch round cutter cut out biscuits. Invert biscuits onto prepared baking pan so that they barely touch one another and let rise, loosely covered, in a warm place 1 hour, or until almost doubled in bulk.

Preheat oven to 425° F.

Brush tops of biscuits with melted butter and bake in middle of oven 15 minutes, or until golden. Makes about 16 biscuits.

more lunch entrées

Butternut Squash Soup with Ginger and Lime
and Asiago Toasts (page 120)

Butternut Squash Soup with Ginger and Lime

For soup

3/4   cup finely chopped onion

2   tablespoons minced peeled fresh gingerroot

1/2   stick (1/4 cup) unsalted butter

6   cups peeled, seeded, and thinly sliced butternut squash (about 2 1/4 pounds)

3   cups chicken broth

4   cups water

4   large garlic cloves

3   tablespoons fresh lime juice, or to taste

For fried ginger

1/2   cup vegetable oil

1/4   cup about 1 1/2-inch-long julienne strips of peeled fresh gingerroot

Garnish: 6 thin decoratively cut lime slices
Accompaniment: Asiago toasts
(recipe follows)

Make soup:

In a large saucepan cook onion and gingerroot in butter over moderately low heat, stirring occasionally, until onion is softened and add squash, broth, water, and garlic. Bring liquid to a boil and simmer, covered, 15 to 20 minutes, or until squash is tender. In a blender or food processor purée mixture in batches, transferring as puréed, to pan and stir in lime juice and salt and pepper to taste. *Soup may be made 2 days ahead and chilled, covered. Reheat soup over moderately low heat until hot.*

Make fried ginger:

In a small skillet heat oil over moderately high heat until hot but not smoking and fry gingerroot, stirring, 1 minute, or until pale golden. Transfer ginger with a slotted spoon to paper towels to drain.

Serve soup, hot or at room temperature, topped with lime slices and fried ginger and serve with Asiago toasts on the side. Serves 6.

Photo on page 118

Asiago Toasts

12   1/4-inch-thick slices whole-wheat French or Italian bread

about 5 tablespoons olive oil or melted unsalted butter

1   cup freshly grated Asiago* or Parmesan cheese

*available at specialty foods shops and some supermarkets

Preheat broiler.

In a shallow baking pan broil bread slices under broiler about 3 inches from heat 1 to 2 minutes, or until tops are golden. Turn slices and brush with oil or butter. Broil slices 30 seconds to 1 minute, or until crisp but not colored. Cover toasts evenly with cheese and broil 1 minute more, or until cheese is melted.

Serve toasts warm or at room temperature. Makes 12 toasts.

Photo on page 118

Curried Chicken Soup

4 cups chicken broth
1 whole boneless skinless chicken breast, halved
2 onions, chopped
1 cup chopped celery including some leaves
1 Golden Delicious apple, peeled and chopped
2 tablespoons vegetable oil
2 tablespoons curry powder, or to taste
2 tablespoons all-purpose flour
1 cup half-and-half

Garnish: golden raisins, plumped in warm water 15 minutes and drained

In a skillet bring 3 cups chicken broth to a boil. Add chicken, reducing heat to keep broth at a bare simmer, and simmer, turning once, 8 minutes, or until springy to the touch. Transfer chicken to a cutting board, reserving broth, and chop.

In a large saucepan cook onions, celery, and apple in oil, covered, over moderately low heat, stirring occasionally, 10 minutes, or until vegetables are softened. Stir in curry powder and cook, stirring, 2 minutes. Stir in flour and cook, stirring, 3 minutes. Stir in remaining 1 cup broth. Bring liquid to a boil and simmer, stirring occasionally, 10 minutes.

In a food processor or blender purée mixture and in a bowl or saucepan combine with reserved broth, chicken, and half-and-half. Chill soup, covered, 3 hours, or until cold, or heat until hot but not boiling.

Serve soup garnished with raisins. Makes about 6 cups, serving 6.

⊕+ Chilled Tomato Basil Soup

2 1/2 pounds vine-ripened tomatoes (about 6), cut into chunks
1 tablespoon cornstarch
1/2 cup beef broth
1 tablespoon fresh lemon juice
1/2 teaspoon sugar
10 fresh basil leaves

Garnish: sour cream, 1/3 cup chopped fresh basil leaves, and extra-virgin olive oil for drizzling soup
Accompaniment: garlic *baguette* toasts (recipe follows)

In a food processor purée tomatoes and force through a fine sieve into a saucepan, pressing hard on solids. In a small bowl stir together cornstarch and broth and stir into purée. Bring mixture to a boil, stirring, and remove pan from heat. Stir in lemon juice, sugar, basil leaves, and salt and pepper to taste and cool soup. *Chill soup, covered, at least 8 hours and up to 2 days.*

Discard basil leaves and serve soup garnished with sour cream, chopped basil, and oil. Serve soup with toasts on the side. Makes about 6 cups, serving 6.

Photo on jacket

◔ Garlic Baguette Toasts

1 large garlic clove, minced
1/4 cup olive oil
1 *baguette*, cut lengthwise into 6 long wedges
coarse salt to taste

Preheat oven to 375° F.

In a small skillet cook garlic in oil over moderate heat, stirring, until it begins to turn golden and brush bread wedges with garlic oil. On a baking sheet bake wedges in middle of oven 10 minutes, or until golden. Sprinkle toasts with salt and break in half. Makes 12 toasts, serving 6.

Photo on jacket

Chilled Buttermilk Bell Pepper Soup

4   cups chopped red bell pepper
2   cups chopped leek (white and
      pale green parts only), washed well
3   tablespoons olive oil
1 1/2   cups chicken broth
3 3/4   cups buttermilk

In a large heavy saucepan sweat bell pepper and leek in oil, covered directly with a buttered round of wax paper and lid, over low heat 15 minutes, or until softened. Discard wax paper and add broth. Bring mixture just to a boil and simmer, partially covered, 30 minutes.

In a food processor or blender purée mixture in batches until smooth, transferring to a bowl as puréed. Cool purée and stir in buttermilk and salt and pepper to taste. *Chill soup, covered, at least 4 hours and up to 1 day.* Makes about 6¼ cups, serving 6.

Roast Beef, Green Bean, Potato, and Blue Cheese Salad

For vinaigrette
1   tablespoon coarse-grain mustard
1   tablespoon Worcestershire sauce
6   tablespoons red-wine vinegar
2/3   cup extra-virgin olive oil

1 1/2   pounds small red potatoes
3   tablespoons minced fresh parsley leaves
1 1/2   pounds green beans, trimmed
3/4   cup crumbled blue cheese
1 1/2   pounds rare roast beef, cut into thin strips
      frisée (curly endive) for lining platter

Make vinaigrette:
In a small bowl combine mustard, Worcestershire sauce, vinegar, and salt and pepper to taste. Add oil in a stream, whisking until emulsified.

In a saucepan combine potatoes with salted cold water to cover by 1 inch. Bring water to a boil and simmer, covered, 15 to 20 minutes, or until potatoes are just tender. Pour off water and steam potatoes, covered, over moderately low heat, shaking pan, 3 minutes. Cool potatoes 10 minutes, or until just cool enough to handle. Quarter warm potatoes and in a bowl toss with one fourth of vinaigrette and parsley. In a large saucepan of salted boiling water cook green beans until just tender, about 3 minutes. Drain beans in a colander and rinse under cold water to stop cooking. Pat beans dry and in a small bowl toss with half of cheese and half of remaining vinaigrette. In another small bowl toss beef with remaining vinaigrette.

Line a large platter with *frisée* and arrange potatoes, beans, and beef in mounds in center. Sprinkle salad with remaining cheese and season with pepper to taste. Serve salad at room temperature. Serves 6.

Chinese Noodle Salad with Poached Chicken Breasts

2	whole boneless skinless chicken breasts (about 1 1/2 pounds)
	For peanut sauce
1/4	cup creamy peanut butter
1/3	cup chicken broth
1/2	cup soy sauce
1 1/2	tablespoons rice vinegar (not seasoned)*
1 1/2	tablespoons Asian sesame oil*
1	tablespoon sugar
1	tablespoon minced garlic
1	tablespoon minced peeled fresh gingerroot
1	teaspoon Tabasco
1	pound dried thin Chinese egg noodles* or thin spaghetti
2	tablespoons vegetable oil
4	teaspoons Asian sesame oil*
1	European cucumber (about 12 inches long), seeded and chopped fine
2	cups coarsely grated carrot (about 4 carrots)

Garnish: 1/2 cup thinly sliced scallion greens

*available at Asian markets and many supermarkets

In a large deep skillet or 4-quart saucepan combine chicken and cold water to cover by 1 inch and remove chicken. Bring water to a boil and add chicken and salt to taste. Poach chicken, uncovered, at a bare simmer 12 minutes. Remove skillet or pan from heat and cool chicken in liquid 30 minutes. Drain chicken and let stand until cool enough to handle. *Chicken may be poached 1 day ahead and chilled, covered.* Slice chicken into strips across grain.

Make peanut sauce:

In a bowl whisk peanut butter and whisk in broth, 1 tablespoon at a time, whisking until smooth after each addition. Whisk in remaining peanut sauce ingredients. *Sauce may be made 1 day ahead and chilled, covered.*

In a kettle bring 3 quarts water to a boil. Add noodles or spaghetti and cook until *al dente.* In a colander drain noodles and rinse under cold water to stop cooking. Drain noodles and transfer to a platter. Toss noodles with vegetable oil and sesame oil.

Arrange chopped cucumber and grated carrot over noodles and top vegetables with chicken. Pour peanut sauce over salad and garnish with scallion greens. Serves 6.

Chicken Taco Salad with Salsa Vinaigrette

For vinaigrette

- 1   large garlic clove, chopped
- 1/3   cup fresh lime juice (about 2 limes)
- 1/2   teaspoon ground cumin, or to taste
- 2   cups chopped seeded vine-ripened tomato (about 1 pound)
- 1   large *jalapeño* chili, seeded and chopped (wear rubber gloves)
- 1/2   cup vegetable oil

- 2   whole skinless boneless chicken breasts (about 1 1/2 pounds)
- 2   teaspoons ground cumin
- 2   teaspoons chili powder
- 1   tablespoon vegetable oil
- 1   head romaine (about 3/4 pound), shredded
- 2   cups julienned peeled *jícama**
- 1/2   pound corn tortilla chips, broken into 1-inch pieces
- 3   cups vine-ripened cherry tomatoes, quartered (about 1 pound)
- 1   cup coarsely grated Cheddar cheese
- 1/3   cup thinly sliced scallion

Garnish: 1/2 cup chopped fresh coriander

*available at specialty produce markets and some supermarkets

Make vinaigrette:
In a blender blend together all vinaigrette ingredients except oil with salt and pepper to taste. With motor running add oil in a stream and blend until emulsified. *Vinaigrette may be made 1 day ahead and chilled, covered.*

Rub chicken with cumin, chili powder, oil, and salt and pepper to taste. In a well-seasoned cast-iron grill pan heated over moderately high heat or on a grill rack set about 6 inches over glowing coals grill chicken 5 to 8 minutes on each side, or until springy to the touch. Transfer chicken to a cutting board and let stand 10 minutes. Slice chicken into thin strips across grain.

Scatter romaine on a large deep platter or in a large bowl and top with chicken and remaining ingredients.

Pour vinaigrette over salad and toss until combined well. (Alternately, transfer vinaigrette to a small bowl and serve on the side.) Garnish salad with coriander. Serves 6.

Scallops and Shrimp in Cucumber Dill Sauce

- 1   cup dry white wine
- 1   cup water
- 1   bay leaf
- 1 1/2   pounds sea or bay scallops
- 1 1/2   pounds medium shrimp, shelled and deveined
- 2   cucumbers, peeled, seeded, chopped fine, and squeezed lightly in a kitchen towel
- 2/3   cup sour cream
- 1/3   cup finely chopped fresh dill
- 2   teaspoons fresh lemon juice
- 2   teaspoons Dijon mustard
- 1/4   teaspoon Tabasco
   soft-leafed lettuce for lining plates

Garnish: cucumber slices and dill sprigs

In a large skillet bring wine and water to a boil with bay leaf and add scallops and shrimp. Simmer seafood, stirring, 2 minutes, or until just cooked through. Drain seafood, discarding bay leaf, and chill, covered, 1 hour, or until cold.

In a bowl stir together remaining ingredients except lettuce with salt and pepper to taste. Add seafood and toss.

Serve mixture on chilled salad plates lined with lettuce and garnish with cucumber and dill. Serves 6.

Potato, Escarole, and Curly Endive Salad with Hot Bacon Dressing

2 1/2 pounds boiling potatoes
3/4 cup dry white wine
1/4 cup chicken broth
1 head escarole (about 3/4 pound),
torn into bite-size pieces
1 head curly endive (about 3/4 pound),
torn into bite-size pieces
3/4 cup minced scallion
2 garlic cloves, minced
1/2 pound thick-cut bacon, cut crosswise
into 1/2-inch pieces
3 tablespoons olive oil
1/2 cup white-wine vinegar

Accompaniments
6 hard-cooked eggs, quartered
1/2 cup minced flat-leafed parsley leaves
24 brine-cured black olives, drained

In a steamer set over boiling water steam potatoes, adding more boiling water if necessary, 15 minutes, or until just tender. Cool potatoes until they can be handled and while warm cut into quarters. In a large bowl toss potatoes gently with ¼ cup wine and broth and let stand, covered, 10 minutes. In a warm large salad bowl combine greens, potato mixture, scallion, and garlic.

In a stainless-steel or enameled skillet cook bacon over moderate heat until brown and crisp and transfer with a slotted spoon to salad bowl. Measure bacon fat and pour off all but ¼ cup. In skillet heat ¼ cup fat and oil until hot. Add fat to salad and toss gently. Add vinegar and remaining ½ cup wine to skillet and boil over high heat until reduced by half. Pour dressing over salad. Toss salad gently and season with salt and pepper to taste.

Serve salad with eggs, parsley, and olives. Serves 6.

Brown Rice and Tuna Salad with Balsamic Vinaigrette

1 2/3 cups long-grain brown rice
For vinaigrette
3 tablespoons balsamic vinegar
2 tablespoons fresh lemon juice
2 teaspoons Dijon mustard
2 teaspoons dried basil, crumbled
1 teaspoon dried oregano, crumbled
1/2 cup olive oil

2 vine-ripened tomatoes, seeded and chopped
1 red bell pepper, chopped
1/2 cup minced shallot or red onion
1 cup chopped celery
2 6-ounce cans solid white tuna
packed in oil, drained
1/2 cup minced flat-leafed parsley leaves

Garnish: lemon wedges

To a 5-quart saucepan of salted boiling water add rice, stirring until water returns to a boil. Boil rice gently 35 minutes and drain in a large sieve set over a large saucepan. Return water to a boil. Rinse rice well and steam in same sieve over boiling water, covered with a paper towel and lid, 10 minutes, or until tender.

Make vinaigrette:

In a small bowl whisk together all vinaigrette ingredients except oil with salt to taste. Add oil in a stream, whisking until emulsified.

In a large bowl combine rice with remaining ingredients and salt and pepper to taste and toss with vinaigrette. *Salad may be made, omitting tuna and parsley, 1 day ahead and chilled, covered. Before serving, add tuna, parsley, and additional balsamic vinegar and lemon juice to taste.*

Serve salad at room temperature and garnish with lemon. Serves 6.

Wheat Berry and Barley Salad with Smoked Mozzarella

1 cup wheat berries*
1 cup pearl barley
1 small red onion, chopped fine
2 garlic cloves, minced and mashed to a paste with 1/2 teaspoon salt
1/4 cup balsamic vinegar
1/4 cup extra-virgin olive oil
6 scallions, chopped fine
1 1/2 cups cooked corn (cut from about 2 large ears)
1/2 pound smoked mozzarella cheese, diced fine
1 pint vine-ripened cherry tomatoes, halved
1/2 cup chopped fresh chives
parsley salad (recipe follows) for lining plates

*available at natural foods stores

Into a kettle of salted boiling water stir wheat berries and boil gently 30 minutes. Stir in barley and boil gently 40 minutes.

While grains are cooking, in a large bowl stir together onion, garlic paste, vinegar, and oil.

Drain grains well and add to onion mixture. Toss mixture well and cool. Add remaining ingredients except parsley salad with salt and pepper to taste and toss well. *Salad may be made 1 day ahead and chilled, covered. Bring salad to room temperature before serving.*

Line plates with parsley salad and top with wheat berry and barley salad. Serves 6.

Photo opposite

Wheat Berry and Barley Salad with Smoked Mozzarella

Parsley Salad

3 cups packed flat-leafed parsley leaves
1 1/2 to 2 tablespoons extra-virgin olive oil
1 teaspoon fresh lemon juice
1/4 teaspoon *umeboshi* vinegar* or salt

*available at natural foods stores

In a bowl toss ingredients together well. Serves 6.

Chicken BLTs

For marinade
3/4 teaspoon salt
3/4 teaspoon cumin
1/2 teaspoon dried thyme, crumbled
1/4 teaspoon black pepper
1/8 teaspoon cayenne
2 tablespoons vegetable oil

2 whole boneless skinless chicken breasts (about 1 1/2 pounds), halved
12 slices bacon
12 1/2-inch-thick slices crusty peasant or Portuguese bread, very lightly toasted
about 1/2 cup mayonnaise
soft-leafed lettuce for sandwiches
3 vine-ripened tomatoes, sliced thin

Make marinade:
In a bowl stir together marinade ingredients.

Add chicken and rub marinade all over it. Marinate chicken while cooking bacon.

In a large heavy skillet cook bacon over moderate heat until crisp and transfer to paper towels to drain. Pour off fat from skillet. Heat skillet over moderately high heat until hot but not smoking and sauté chicken until cooked through, about 5 minutes on each side. Transfer chicken to a cutting board and let stand 5 minutes. Cut chicken across grain into thin slices.

Spread toast with mayonnaise and layer with lettuce, tomatoes, bacon, and chicken to make sandwiches. Serves 6.

⊙+ Greek-Style Lamb Burgers with Minted Yogurt Sauce

For yogurt sauce
1   12-ounce container plain yogurt
2   small garlic cloves, minced and mashed to a paste with 1/4 teaspoon salt
3   tablespoons shredded fresh mint leaves, or to taste
For burgers
2   pounds ground lamb
1/2 cup crumbled feta cheese
1/2 cup finely chopped pitted Kalamata olives (12 to 15)

6   small pita loaves, each split halfway around edge to form a pocket
2   small vine-ripened tomatoes, sliced
2   small green bell peppers, cut into rings
1   red onion, sliced thin

Make yogurt sauce:
Drain yogurt in a sieve lined with a dampened paper towel set over a bowl 30 minutes. Transfer drained yogurt to a small bowl and stir in garlic paste and mint.

Make burgers:
Prepare grill.

Handling lamb as gently as possible, in a bowl combine lamb with feta and olives and form into six 1-inch-thick patties. Season burgers lightly with salt and pepper to taste and grill on an oiled rack set 5 to 6 inches over glowing coals 7 minutes on each side for medium-rare.

Transfer burgers to pita pockets and top with tomatoes, bell peppers, and onion. Serve burgers with yogurt sauce. Serves 6.

Photo on page 130

⊙+ Thai-Style Turkey Burgers with Pickled Cucumbers

For pickled cucumbers
1/2 cup distilled white vinegar
2 1/2 tablespoons firmly packed light brown sugar
1 1/4 teaspoons salt
3/4 teaspoon dried hot red pepper flakes
1   seedless cucumber (about 1 pound), sliced very thin
For burgers
2   garlic cloves
1 1/2 teaspoons finely chopped peeled fresh gingerroot
1/2 cup chopped fresh coriander
1/2 cup chopped fresh mint leaves
1/2 cup chopped fresh basil leaves
3   tablespoons fresh lime juice
3   teaspoons sugar
2   flat anchovy fillets
2   pounds ground turkey
1/4 cup fresh bread crumbs
1/4 teaspoon cayenne, or to taste

4   sesame hamburger buns or onion rolls, split and toasted

Make pickled cucumbers:
In a small bowl stir together all pickled cucumber ingredients except cucumber until sugar and salt are dissolved. Add cucumber, stirring to coat well, and marinate 30 minutes.

Make burgers:
Prepare grill.

Into a food processor with motor running, drop garlic and gingerroot. Add coriander, mint, basil, lime juice, sugar, and anchovy fillets and blend well. In a bowl combine well turkey, herb mixture, bread crumbs, and cayenne and form into six 1-inch-thick patties. Season burgers with salt and pepper to taste and grill on an oiled rack set 5 to 6 inches over glowing coals 6 minutes on each side, or until just cooked through.

Drain cucumbers. Transfer burgers to buns or rolls and top with pickled cucumbers. Serves 6.

Photo on page 130

Barbecue Pork Burgers with Coleslaw

For barbecue sauce

2/3	cup minced onion
3	garlic cloves, minced
3	tablespoons unsalted butter
1 1/2	cups ketchup
4 1/2	tablespoons Worcestershire sauce
3	teaspoons dry mustard
1/3	cup cider vinegar
1/3	cup firmly packed brown sugar
3 3/4	teaspoons chili powder
3/4	teaspoon Tabasco

For coleslaw

3	cups thinly shredded cabbage
1/2	cup coarsely grated carrot
1/3	cup thinly sliced red onion
1	tablespoon fresh lemon juice, or to taste
1/3	cup mayonnaise, or to taste

2	pounds ground pork
1/4	cup fresh bread crumbs
6	sesame hamburger buns, split and toasted

Make barbecue sauce:

In a heavy saucepan cook onion and garlic in butter over moderately low heat, stirring, until onion is softened. Add remaining barbecue sauce ingredients and simmer, stirring occasionally, 15 minutes. Transfer barbecue sauce to a bowl and cool. *Barbecue sauce may be made 4 days ahead and chilled, covered.*

Make coleslaw:

In a bowl stir together well coleslaw ingredients and salt and pepper to taste.

Prepare grill.

In a bowl combine well pork, bread crumbs, and ½ cup barbecue sauce and form into six ¾-inch-thick patties. Reserve ½ cup barbecue sauce in a bowl. Season burgers with salt and pepper to taste and grill on an oiled rack set 5 to 6 inches over glowing coals, basting often with remaining barbecue sauce and turning several times, until just cooked through, about 5 minutes on each side.

Transfer burgers to buns and top with coleslaw. Serve reserved barbecue sauce on the side. Serves 6.

Photo on page 130

Saga Blue, Walnut, and Apple Tea Sandwiches

1/2 pound Saga blue cheese, rind discarded
      and cheese softened
  2 ounces cream cheese, softened
  6 tablespoons chopped walnuts
 12 slices dark pumpernickel bread
  1 to 2 firm tart apples (such as Granny Smith)
  1 bunch watercress, stems discarded
      and sprigs rinsed and spun dry

In a bowl with a fork blend together cheeses, nuts, and salt and pepper to taste until smooth.

Spread bread with cheese mixture. Peel apples and slice thin. Top half of bread slices with a layer of apple and top with watercress. Top watercress with remaining bread slices and press together gently. Trim crusts and cut sandwiches into quarters. *Sandwiches may be made 1 hour ahead and chilled, wrapped in plastic wrap.* Makes 24 sandwiches.

Tomato, Olive, and Basil Pita Pizzas

  3 6-inch pita loaves, split horizontally
  2 cups grated mozzarella cheese
      (about 6 ounces)
  2 vine-ripened tomatoes, seeded
      and sliced very thin
  1 cup Kalamata or other brine-cured black
      olives, pitted and sliced
  1 tablespoon minced garlic
      freshly ground black pepper to taste
1/4 cup extra-virgin olive oil
  1 cup thinly sliced fresh basil leaves

Preheat oven to 375° F.

Arrange pita rounds, rough sides up, on 2 large baking sheets and toast in oven 3 minutes, or until crisp but not colored. Top pitas with mozzarella, tomatoes, olives, garlic, pepper, and salt to taste. Drizzle pizzas with oil and bake in middle of oven 8 minutes. Sprinkle basil over pizzas and bake 2 to 5 minutes more, or until edges are golden brown.

Serve pizzas cut into wedges, preferably with a pizza wheel. Serves 6.

**Barbecue Pork Burger with Coleslaw;
Thai-Style Turkey Burger with Pickled Cucumbers; and
Greek-Style Lamb Burger with Minted Yogurt Sauce
(pages 128 to 129)**

The following pizza can be made with 1 3/4 to 2 pounds store-bought pizza dough, available at some pizzerias, pasta shops, and supermarkets.

Double-Crust Pizza with Sausage Stuffing

2 1/4-ounce packages active dry yeast (5 teaspoons)
1 1/2 cups lukewarm water
1 teaspoon sugar
4 cups all-purpose flour
5 tablespoons olive oil
1 tablespoon salt
2 onions, sliced thin
2 green and/or red bell peppers, sliced thin
1 1/4 pounds hot Italian sausage, casings discarded
2 large garlic cloves, minced
1 32-ounce can whole tomatoes, drained well and chopped
1/2 cup dry white wine
3/4 teaspoon dried oregano, crumbled
1 teaspoon crushed fennel seed
3 cups finely diced mozzarella cheese (about 12 ounces)
3 tablespoons bread crumbs, toasted

In a large bowl proof yeast in lukewarm water with sugar until foamy, about 5 minutes. Add flour, 2 tablespoons oil, and salt and combine well. On a floured surface knead dough 5 minutes, or until smooth and elastic, and form into a ball. Put dough in an oiled deep bowl, turning to coat. Cover dough loosely and let rise in a warm place 1½ hours, or until doubled in bulk. *(Alternately, dough may be allowed to rise, covered, in refrigerator overnight.)*

In a stainless-steel or enameled skillet cook onions in remaining 3 tablespoons oil over moderate heat, stirring, until softened. Add bell peppers, and cook, stirring, until onion is golden. Add sausage and garlic and cook, stirring, until meat is no longer pink. Add tomatoes, wine, oregano, and fennel seed and simmer, stirring, until excess liquid is evaporated. Transfer mixture to a bowl and cool. Stir in mozzarella and salt and pepper to taste. *Filling may be made 1 day ahead and chilled, covered.*

Preheat oven to 400° F.

Punch down dough and halve it. Reserve half of dough under an inverted bowl and on a floured surface roll remaining half into a 16- by 14-inch oval. Transfer oval to a large baking sheet and sprinkle evenly with bread crumbs, leaving a 1-inch border. Spread filling over bread crumbs. On a floured surface roll reserved dough into a 16- by 14-inch oval and drape over filling. Pinch edges together to seal in filling and brush top lightly with water. Bake pizza in upper third of oven 35 minutes, or until crust is golden brown and sounds hollow when tapped. Transfer pizza with spatulas to a rack and cool 5 minutes. *Pizza may be made 1 week ahead and cooled completely, uncovered, before freezing, wrapped in plastic wrap. Reheat frozen pizza in a 400° F. oven 20 minutes, or until heated through.* Serves 6.

Swiss Chard Pie with Ricotta, Sausage, and Pine Nuts

- 1 1/2 **pounds Swiss chard, ribs cut out and reserved and leaves washed well and spun dry**
- 2 **cups chopped onion**
- 2 **garlic cloves, minced**
- 2 **tablespoons olive oil**
- 1/2 **pound hot Italian sausage, casings discarded**
- 1 1/2 **cups whole-milk ricotta cheese (about 15 ounces), drained in a fine sieve set over a bowl, 1 hour**
- 2 **large eggs, beaten lightly**
- 3 **tablespoons pine nuts, toasted lightly**
- 1/2 **cup freshly grated Parmesan cheese**
- 1 **recipe egg pastry dough (recipe follows)**

Finely chop reserved Swiss chard ribs and shred or chop leaves. In a large skillet cook onion and garlic in oil over moderately low heat, stirring occasionally, until they begin to turn golden. Add chard ribs and cook, covered, stirring occasionally, 5 minutes. Add chard leaves and salt to taste and cook, covered, 3 minutes, or until wilted. Remove lid and cook over moderate heat, stirring, 3 to 5 minutes, or until all liquid is evaporated. In another skillet cook sausage over moderate heat, stirring and breaking up lumps, until lightly browned and transfer to paper towels to drain well. Stir sausage into chard mixture and cool. Add ricotta, eggs, pine nuts, Parmesan, and salt and pepper to taste and stir until combined well.

Preheat oven to 400° F.

On a lightly floured surface roll out half of dough ⅛ inch thick and fit into a tart pan with a removable fluted rim, 10 inches across bottom and 1 inch deep. Trim edge, leaving a ½-inch overhang. On a lightly floured surface roll out remaining dough ⅛ inch thick. Spread filling evenly in shell. Cover filling with rolled-out dough and trim edge, leaving a ¾-inch overhang. Fold top overhang under bottom overhang, tucking it inside rim and crimping edge decoratively to seal. Prick top crust all over with a fork and bake in upper third of oven 45 to 50 minutes, or until golden. Cool pie in pan on a rack. *Pie may be made 1 day ahead and chilled, covered. Reheat pie in a 350° F. oven until heated through, about 10 minutes.*

Serve pie warm or at room temperature. Serves 6.

◐+ Egg Pastry Dough

- 1 **large egg**
- 1 **large egg yolk**
- 2 1/2 **cups plus 2 tablespoons all-purpose flour**
- 1/2 **teaspoon salt**
- 1 1/2 **sticks (3/4 cup) cold unsalted butter, cut into bits**
- 5 **to 7 tablespoons ice water**

In a small bowl beat lightly whole egg and yolk. In another bowl blend together flour, salt, and butter until mixture resembles coarse meal and toss in beaten egg and enough ice water to just form a dough. On a work surface knead dough lightly with heel of hand, distributing butter evenly, for a few seconds. Form dough into a ball and flatten into a disk. *Chill dough, wrapped in plastic wrap, at least 1 hour or overnight.*

Niçoise Onion Tart

1/2	pound puff pastry dough (1 sheet), thawed if frozen
2	pounds onions, sliced thin (about 7 cups)
1/4	cup plus 2 tablespoons olive oil
1	28-ounce can whole Italian tomatoes, drained and chopped coarse
2	large garlic cloves, minced
1	teaspoon dried thyme, crumbled
1	teaspoon dried rosemary, crumbled
1	bay leaf
3	tablespoons dry bread crumbs
1/4	cup freshly grated Parmesan cheese
2	2-ounce cans flat anchovy fillets, drained about 15 Niçoise olives, pitted and halved

On a floured surface roll pastry into an 18- by 13-inch rectangle. Fit pastry into a shallow baking pan, 15½ by 10½ by 1 inch, and crimp edge decoratively. Prick bottom of shell all over with a fork and freeze 15 minutes.

In a large heavy stainless-steel or enameled skillet sweat onions in ¼ cup oil, covered directly with a round of wax paper and lid, over low heat, stirring occasionally, 30 minutes. Discard wax paper. Add tomatoes, garlic, herbs, and salt and pepper to taste and cook, covered, over low heat 10 minutes. Remove lid and cook filling over moderately high heat, stirring, 10 minutes more, or until most liquid is evaporated. Discard bay leaf and cool. *Filling may be made 1 day ahead and chilled, covered.*

Preheat oven to 425° F.

Sprinkle bread crumbs in bottom of shell and spread filling evenly in shell. Sprinkle filling with Parmesan and arrange anchovy fillets and olives decoratively on top. Freeze tart 5 minutes. Drizzle tart with remaining 2 tablespoons oil and bake in lower third of oven 30 to 40 minutes, or until crust is golden brown.

Cut tart into squares. Serves 6.

Squash, Pepper Jack, and Basil Quiche

1	recipe pastry dough (page 23) raw rice for weighting shell
1	pound mixed summer squash and zucchini
1	teaspoon salt
1	cup grated pepper Jack cheese (about 4 ounces)
1/4	cup freshly grated Parmesan cheese
1 1/4	cups half-and-half
2	large eggs
1/2	cup chopped fresh basil leaves
1/2	teaspoon dried oregano, crumbled

Preheat oven to 425° F.

On a lightly floured surface roll out dough ⅛ inch thick. Fit dough into a 1-quart metal pie pan, 9 inches across top and 1¼ inches deep, and crimp edge decoratively. Prick bottom of shell lightly all over with a fork and chill 30 minutes or freeze 15 minutes. *Shell may be made 2 days ahead and chilled, covered.* Line shell with wax paper and fill with rice. Bake shell in middle of oven 10 minutes. Remove rice and paper carefully and bake shell 5 to 6 minutes more, or until golden. Cool shell in pan on a rack.

Reduce temperature to 375° F.

Coarsely grate all squash. In a colander toss squash with salt and drain squash 30 minutes.

Pat squash dry with paper towels, pressing out excess liquid, and in a bowl toss with cheeses. Spread mixture evenly in shell. In a bowl whisk together remaining ingredients with salt and pepper to taste and pour into shell. Bake quiche in middle of oven 30 to 35 minutes, or until a knife inserted in custard ½ inch from edge comes out clean. Cool quiche at least 20 minutes. *Quiche may be made 1 day ahead and chilled, covered. Reheat quiche in a 375° F. oven until heated through, about 10 minutes.*

Serve quiche warm or at room temperature. Serves 6.

Baked Parmesan Chicken Wings

3 pounds chicken wings
For marinade
3/4 cup plain yogurt
1/4 cup fresh lemon juice
1 1/2 tablespoons Dijon mustard
3 garlic cloves, minced
1 teaspoon salt
1/2 teaspoon dried sage, crumbled
1/2 teaspoon dried oregano, crumbled

3/4 cup dry bread crumbs
3/4 cup freshly grated Parmesan cheese
cayenne to taste
melted unsalted butter for drizzling wings

Cut off chicken wing tips and reserve for another use if desired. Halve wings at joints.

Make marinade:

In a ceramic or glass bowl stir together marinade ingredients with pepper to taste.

Add wings to marinade and toss to coat. *Marinate wings, covered, at room temperature 2 hours or chilled overnight.*

Butter generously a shallow baking pan.

In a plastic or paper bag combine bread crumbs, Parmesan, cayenne, and salt and black pepper to taste. Drain wings and shake, a few at a time, with bread crumb mixture, coating well. Arrange wings as coated 1 inch apart on prepared baking pan and chill 1 hour.

Preheat oven to 375° F.

Drizzle chicken wings with butter and bake in middle of oven 30 minutes, or until golden brown. Serves 6.

☺+ Tomatoes Stuffed with Herbed Orzo and Ricotta Salata

6 3/4-pound vine-ripened tomatoes
1/4 cup olive oil plus additional for brushing tomatoes
1/3 cup *orzo* (rice-shaped pasta)
3/4 cup crumbled *ricotta salata* (firm salted sheep's milk cheese)
1/3 cup Kalamata or other brine-cured black olives, pitted and quartered
2 tablespoons minced fresh oregano leaves
1/2 cup finely chopped fresh parsley leaves
2 teaspoons minced fresh dill
2 tablespoons fresh lemon juice

Preheat oven to 325° F. and lightly oil a shallow baking dish.

Core and cut ½-inch slices from stem ends of tomatoes, reserving slices. With a small spoon remove and discard seeds and liquid without squeezing tomatoes. Remove remaining pulp, reserving it and leaving ½-inch shell. Sprinkle insides of tomatoes with salt and pepper to taste and brush with additional oil. Arrange tomatoes, cut ends up, in prepared baking dish and bake in middle of oven 15 minutes. Invert tomatoes on a rack and drain 30 minutes. Chop reserved tomato slices and pulp and put in a bowl.

In a saucepan of salted boiling water cook *orzo*, stirring once or twice, 8 minutes, or until tender, and drain. Add *orzo* to chopped tomato with remaining ingredients, remaining ¼ cup oil, and salt and pepper to taste and toss to combine. *Filling may be made 4 hours ahead and chilled, covered.*

Divide filling among tomatoes, mounding it. Serve tomatoes at room temperature. Serves 6.

more
dinner
entrées

Tomato Phyllo Pizza (page 150)

Korean-Style Beef Kebabs with Scallions and Broccoli

1　pound broccoli, cut into 2-inch flowerets, reserving stems for another use
　　For marinade
5　garlic cloves, forced through a garlic press or minced
1/2　cup soy sauce
3　tablespoons Asian sesame oil*
2　teaspoons minced peeled fresh gingerroot
3　tablespoons sugar
2　teaspoons distilled white vinegar
2　teaspoons sesame seeds
1　teaspoon freshly ground black pepper

2　pounds boneless top round beef, cut into 1 1/2-inch cubes
　　white parts of 18 scallions, trimmed
8　12-inch bamboo skewers

　　*available at Asian markets and some supermarkets

In a large saucepan of boiling salted water blanch broccoli 2 minutes. Drain broccoli and plunge into a bowl of ice and cold water to stop cooking.

Make marinade:

In a large bowl whisk together well marinade ingredients.

Add beef to marinade, coating well, and transfer to a large resealable plastic bag. Add scallions and broccoli and any remaining marinade to bag and seal. *Marinate mixture, chilled, turning bag occasionally, overnight.*

In a shallow dish soak skewers in water to cover 1 hour.

Prepare grill.

Thread beef onto some skewers and thread vegetables onto remaining skewers. Discard marinade. Grill beef kebabs on an oiled rack set 5 to 6 inches over glowing coals 5 to 7 minutes on each side for medium-rare. Grill vegetable kebabs, turning occasionally, 4 minutes, or until just browned. Serves 6.

☺+ Garlic and Cumin Marinated Flank Steak

2　to 2 1/2 pounds flank steak
　　For marinade
3　tablespoons fresh lemon juice
1/3　cup vegetable oil
3　garlic cloves, minced and mashed to a paste with 1/2 teaspoon salt
2　teaspoons ground cumin
1/2　cup chopped fresh coriander
1/4　cup dry vermouth
1　teaspoon freshly ground black pepper

Garnish: chopped fresh coriander

In a shallow ceramic or glass dish large enough to hold steak or in a large resealable plastic bag combine well marinade ingredients and add steak, coating well. *Marinate steak, covered or sealed in bag and chilled, turning occasionally, at least 6 hours or overnight.*

Prepare grill.

Discard marinade and grill steak on an oiled rack set about 6 inches over glowing coals 5 minutes on each side for medium-rare.

Transfer steak to a cutting board and holding a knife at a 45° angle slice it thin across grain.

Garnish steak with coriander. Serves 6.

Lamb and Zucchini Kebabs with Lemon Tarragon Marinade

For marinade
1   cup vegetable oil
1/3 cup fresh lemon juice
3   scallions, sliced thin
2   teaspoons tarragon mustard or
    Dijon mustard
2   teaspoons dried tarragon, crumbled
1   teaspoon salt

2   pounds boneless lamb shoulder or leg,
    trimmed and cut into 1 1/2-inch cubes
3   zucchini (about 1 1/2 pounds),
    cut into 1-inch pieces
8   12-inch bamboo skewers

Garnish: about 1 tablespoon minced
fresh tarragon leaves

Make marinade:
In a shallow ceramic or glass dish combine marinade ingredients.

Add lamb and zucchini to marinade, coating well. *Marinate lamb and zucchini, covered and chilled, tossing occasionally, at least 6 hours or overnight.*

In a shallow dish soak skewers in water to cover 1 hour.

Prepare grill.

Discard marinade and thread lamb and zucchini alternately onto skewers. Grill kebabs on an oiled rack set about 4 inches over glowing coals, turning occasionally, 15 to 20 minutes for medium-rare.

Garnish kebabs with tarragon. Serves 6.

Cider-Braised Pork Loin

1   teaspoon salt
1   teaspoon freshly ground black pepper
2   teaspoons dried sage, crumbled
1   3-pound rib-end boneless pork loin,
    rolled and tied
2   tablespoons olive oil
1   Granny Smith apple, cored and chopped
2   onions, sliced
3   garlic cloves
1   bay leaf
2   cups apple cider
1   cup water
1/2 cup dry white wine
2   tablespoons cider vinegar

In a small bowl combine salt, pepper, and sage and rub on pork. *Wrap pork in wax paper and chill at least 2 hours or overnight.*

Preheat oven to 325° F.

In an ovenproof kettle heat oil over moderately high heat until hot but not smoking and brown pork on all sides. Transfer pork to a plate. In oil remaining in kettle cook apple and onions over moderate heat, stirring, until they begin to brown. Add remaining ingredients and bring to a boil. Return pork to kettle and braise, covered, in oven about 1 hour and 15 minutes or until a meat thermometer registers 155° F.

Transfer pork to a platter and let stand, covered. Skim fat from cooking liquid and discard bay leaf. In a blender or food processor purée cooking liquid and solids in batches, transferring sauce to a saucepan, and simmer 10 minutes, or until reduced to about 2 cups.

Season sauce with salt and pepper and serve with pork. Serves 6.

Pork Chops with Creamy Mustard Chive Sauce

1 1/2   tablespoons olive oil
    6   3/4-inch-thick loin pork chops
    1   small onion, chopped
    2   teaspoons all-purpose flour
  1/3   cup dry white wine
    1   teaspoon cider vinegar
  1/2   cup heavy cream
  1/3   cup chicken broth
    2   tablespoons coarse-grained Dijon mustard
    2   tablespoons minced fresh chives

Preheat oven to 200° F.

In a large heavy skillet heat oil over moderately high heat until hot but not smoking and sauté chops, in batches if necessary, patted dry and seasoned with salt and pepper, turning once, 8 to 10 minutes, or until cooked through. Transfer chops to an ovenproof platter and keep warm in oven.

In oil remaining in skillet cook onion over moderate heat, stirring, 1 minute and stir in flour. Cook mixture, stirring, 1 minute and stir in wine and vinegar, scraping up brown bits. Simmer mixture 2 minutes and whisk in remaining ingredients, any juices that have accumulated on platter, and salt and pepper to taste.

Spoon sauce over chops. Serves 6.

Braised Chicken with Green Chilies and Tomatoes

    2   tablespoons olive oil
    2   3- to 4-pound chickens,
        cut into serving pieces
    3   onions, chopped
    4   garlic cloves, minced
    1   33 1/2- to 35-ounce can whole
        tomatoes including juice
    2   4 1/2-ounce cans chopped mild green
        chilies, drained
    3   pickled *jalapeño* chilies, seeded
        and chopped (wear rubber gloves)
    1   12-ounce bottle of beer (not dark)
    1   cup chicken broth
    2   teaspoons dried oregano, crumbled
1 1/2   teaspoons ground cumin
    1   tablespoon Worcestershire sauce

Accompaniment: steamed rice (page 169)

In a large heavy kettle heat oil over moderately high heat until hot but not smoking and brown chicken in batches, patted dry and seasoned with salt and pepper, transferring it as browned to a bowl. Pour off all but 2 tablespoons fat and cook onions and garlic over moderately low heat, stirring, until softened. Return chicken and any juices that have accumulated in bowl to kettle and add remaining ingredients and salt and pepper to taste. Bring liquid to a boil and simmer, covered, 45 minutes to 1 hour, or until chicken is tender. Transfer chicken with a slotted spoon to a heated platter and simmer sauce until reduced to about 6 cups. *Chicken and sauce may be made 1 day ahead and cooled completely before chilling separately, covered. Reheat chicken and sauce together over moderate heat, stirring.*

Serve chicken over steamed rice with sauce. Serves 6.

Sesame Chicken with Pineapple

1   3- to 3 1/2-pound chicken,
cut into small serving pieces

1   tablespoon cornstarch plus
additional for dredging
vegetable oil for deep frying

1 1/4 cups chicken broth

2   tablespoons soy sauce

1   tablespoon rice vinegar* (not seasoned)
or distilled white vinegar

1/2 teaspoon dry mustard

1   tablespoon minced peeled fresh gingerroot

1   tablespoon minced garlic

    white part of 1 bunch scallions, minced

1   onion, chopped

1   green bell pepper, sliced

2   cups cubed pineapple (about 1/2 pound)

1   tablespoon sesame seeds, toasted

2   teaspoons Asian sesame oil* if desired

Garnish: 2 inches of green parts of
1 bunch scallions, sliced thin
Accompaniment: steamed rice (page 169)

*available at Asian markets and some
supermarkets

Cut off wing tips and discard or reserve for another use. Cut each breast half, thigh, and drumstick in half through bones. Season chicken with salt and pepper and dredge in cornstarch, shaking off excess.

In a large deep stainless-steel or enameled skillet or a wok fry chicken in batches in 2 inches 375° F. vegetable oil 3 minutes on each side, or until cooked through, transferring with tongs as fried to a plate lined with paper towels. (Make sure oil returns to 375° F. before adding each new batch.) In a small bowl stir together broth, soy sauce, vinegar, remaining 1 tablespoon cornstarch, and mustard.

Pour off all but 2 tablespoons oil from skillet or wok and stir-fry gingerroot, garlic, and white part of scallions over moderately high heat 30 seconds. Add onion, green pepper, and salt and pepper to taste and stir-fry 2 minutes. Add pineapple. Stir cornstarch mixture and add to skillet or wok. Simmer mixture, covered, 3 minutes. Add chicken and sesame seeds and cook over moderate heat, stirring, until heated through. Stir in sesame oil.

Serve chicken mixture, garnished with scallion greens, with rice. Serves 6.

Roasted Chicken and Celery with Anise Sauce

2   3 1/2-pound chickens
2   tablespoons unsalted butter, softened
1   cup dry white wine
3/4 cup water
5   cups 1-inch pieces celery (about 5 ribs)
1   cup chopped onion
3/4 teaspoon dried thyme, crumbled
2   tablespoons anise-flavored liqueur
    such as Pernod or Ricard

Preheat oven to 400° F.

Rinse chickens inside and out and pat completely dry with paper towels. Truss chickens. On a rack in a large flameproof roasting pan arrange chickens, breast sides up, and rub with butter and salt and pepper to taste. Add wine, water, celery, onion, and thyme to pan and roast chickens in middle of oven, basting with pan juices every 15 minutes, about 1 hour and 15 minutes, or until a meat thermometer inserted in fleshy part of a thigh registers 180° F.

Transfer chickens and celery to a platter and keep warm, covered loosely. Add liqueur to pan and bring to a boil over high heat, stirring and scraping up brown bits, until reduced to about 1 cup.

Season sauce with salt and pepper to taste and spoon over celery. Serves 6.

Grilled Turkey Cutlets with Cranberry Jícama Salsa

For salsa
2 1/4 cups diced peeled *jícama** (about 1 pound)
2/3 cup coarsely chopped dried cranberries*
4 1/2 tablespoons pine nuts, lightly toasted
1   large pickled *jalapeño* chili, seeded
    and minced (wear rubber gloves)
3   scallions, minced
1 1/2 tablespoons fresh lime juice
3   tablespoons vegetable oil

2 1/2 pounds 1/2-inch-thick turkey breast cutlets
1/3 cup vegetable oil

    *available at specialty foods shops
    and some supermarkets

Make salsa:

In a small bowl stir together *salsa* ingredients with salt to taste. Salsa *may be made 1 day ahead and chilled, covered.*

Prepare grill.

Pound cutlets between sheets of wax paper until flattened to ¾ inch thick. Brush cutlets with oil and season with salt and pepper to taste. Grill cutlets on a rack set about 4 inches over glowing coals 30 seconds to 1 minute on each side, or until just cooked through.

Serve cutlets with *salsa*. Serves 6.

Cod with Orange and Fennel

- 1 cup thinly sliced shallot
- 3 tablespoons unsalted butter
- 1/4 teaspoon freshly grated orange zest
- 1/2 cup fresh orange juice
- 1/2 cup dry white wine
- 1 teaspoon fennel seeds, bruised with side of a knife
- 2 1/4 pounds cod or halibut fillet, cut into 6 equal portions

Garnish: minced fresh parsley leaves

In a heavy skillet cook shallot in 1 tablespoon butter over moderately low heat until softened. Add zest, orange juice, wine, and fennel seeds and boil, stirring occasionally, until reduced by half. Season fish with salt and pepper. Arrange fish in one layer over sauce and cook, covered, at a bare simmer 10 minutes, or until cooked through.

With a slotted spatula divide fish among 6 heated plates. Bring sauce to a boil and whisk in remaining 2 tablespoons butter and salt and pepper to taste.

Spoon sauce over fish and garnish with parsley. Serves 6.

Flounder Fillets with Snow Peas and Ginger Sauce

- 1/2 cup sliced scallion
- 2 garlic cloves, minced
- 2 teaspoons minced peeled fresh gingerroot
- 5 tablespoons vegetable oil plus additional if necessary
- 1/2 cup water
- 2 tablespoons soy sauce
- 1/4 cup medium-dry Sherry
- 1/2 pound snow peas, cut into 1/4-inch pieces
- 1/2 teaspoon sugar
- 1/2 teaspoon salt
- 6 6-ounce flounder fillets, skinned cornstarch for dredging

Accompaniment: lemon wedges

In a small skillet cook scallion, garlic, and gingerroot in 2 tablespoons oil over moderate heat, stirring, 3 minutes, or until scallion is just softened, and transfer to a bowl with water, soy sauce, Sherry, snow peas, sugar, and salt.

Season flounder with salt to taste and dredge in cornstarch, shaking off excess. In a large stainless-steel or enameled skillet sauté flounder in remaining 3 tablespoons oil, adding more as necessary, over moderately high heat 1½ minutes on each side, or until light golden. Add snow pea mixture and cook, shaking skillet, 1 minute, or until snow peas are crisp-tender.

Transfer flounder with a slotted spatula to a platter and pour sauce over it. Serve fish with lemon wedges. Serves 6.

◑+ Grilled Mako Teriyaki

For marinade

- 1/3 cup soy sauce
- 2 quarter-size slices peeled fresh gingerroot, flattened with side of a cleaver
- 2 tablespoons medium-dry Sherry
- 1 tablespoon sugar
- 1 garlic clove, minced

- 6 6-ounce mako or swordfish steaks, each about 1 inch thick

Garnish: watercress sprigs

Make marinade:

In a small saucepan combine all marinade ingredients and bring to a boil over moderate heat, stirring until sugar is dissolved. Cool marinade.

In a large resealable plastic bag or in a ceramic or glass shallow dish combine marinade and fish and marinate in one layer, chilled, turning, 2 hours.

Prepare grill or preheat broiler and oil rack of grill or broiler pan.

Drain fish, reserving marinade, and let it come to room temperature. Discard gingerroot and in a saucepan boil reserved marinade until reduced by half.

Brush fish with marinade and grill 6 inches over glowing coals or broil under broiler about 6 inches from heat 5 minutes. Turn fish carefully and brush with marinade. Grill or broil fish 5 minutes more, or until cooked through.

Garnish fish with watercress. Serves 6.

◔ Baked Shrimp with Spinach and Feta

- 1 1/2 pounds spinach, washed well
- 1/2 cup chopped shallot
- 1 tablespoon olive oil
- 2 garlic cloves, minced
- 3 tablespoons chopped Kalamata olives
- 3/4 teaspoon dried oregano, crumbled
- 1 cup crumbled feta cheese (about 6 ounces)
- 1 tablespoon fresh lemon juice
- 2 pounds large shrimp (about 40), shelled and deveined

Preheat oven to 450° F. and lightly oil a 13- by 9-inch baking dish.

In a large saucepan cook spinach with water clinging to its leaves, covered, over moderate heat 1 minute, or until wilted, and drain well. Squeeze spinach to remove most of water and chop coarse. In a skillet cook shallot in oil over moderate heat, stirring occasionally, until softened. Add garlic and cook, stirring, 1 minute. Remove skillet from heat and stir in spinach, olives, oregano, feta, and lemon juice, combining well. Spread shrimp in prepared dish and top with spinach mixture. *Shrimp and topping may be made up to this point, 2 hours ahead and chilled, covered.* Bake shrimp in middle of oven 8 to 10 minutes, or until just cooked through. Serves 6.

Shrimp Caesar Salad

- 2 tablespoons olive oil
- 2 1/2 pounds large shrimp (about 50), shelled and deveined
- 1/4 teaspoon cayenne
  For croutons
- 4 cups 1/2-inch cubes fresh French or Italian bread (about 1/2 loaf)
- 2 tablespoons olive oil
  For dressing
- 2 large garlic cloves, chopped
- 3 teaspoons anchovy paste
- 3 tablespoons fresh lemon juice, or to taste
- 1 teaspoon Dijon mustard
- 2 teaspoons Worcestershire sauce
- 1/2 teaspoon salt, or to taste
- 1/2 cup olive oil

- 2 medium heads romaine lettuce, trimmed and torn into bite-size pieces (about 16 cups)
- 1/3 cup freshly grated Parmesan cheese, or to taste

In a large heavy skillet heat oil over moderately high heat until hot but not smoking and sauté shrimp with cayenne and salt and pepper to taste in 2 batches, stirring, until cooked through, about 3 minutes, transferring as cooked with a slotted spoon to a bowl. *Shrimp may be cooked 1 day ahead and chilled, covered. Let shrimp come to room temperature before serving.*

Make croutons:

Preheat oven to 350° F.

In a bowl toss bread cubes with oil and salt to taste and spread in a shallow baking pan. Bake croutons in middle of oven until golden, 10 to 15 minutes.

Make dressing:

In a blender blend together all dressing ingredients except oil until smooth. With motor running add oil in a slow stream and blend until emulsified.

In a large bowl toss romaine with dressing, Parmesan, croutons, and pepper to taste.

Serve salad topped with shrimp. Serves 6.

Marinated Seafood and Blood Orange Salad

3 2 1/2- by 1/2-inch strips of blood orange zest, removed with a vegetable peeler

1 2 1/2- by 1/2-inch strip of lemon zest, removed with a vegetable peeler

12 coriander sprigs

2 quarter-size slices fresh gingerroot

6 whole black peppercorns

1/2 teaspoon salt

4 cups water

1 1/4 pounds large shrimp (about 25), shelled and deveined

1 1/4 pounds sea scallops, halved horizontally if large

5 blood oranges plus 1/3 cup blood orange juice

1/3 cup fresh lime juice

For Maltaise mayonnaise

2/3 cup mayonnaise

1 tablespoon blood orange juice

1 tablespoon fresh lime juice

1 teaspoon Dijon mustard

1/4 teaspoon minced garlic if desired

1/4 teaspoon crushed fresh gingerroot (forced through a garlic press) if desired

2/3 cup minced red or green bell pepper

1/2 cup minced red onion or scallion

1 1/2 tablespoons minced fresh coriander red-leaf lettuce leaves for lining platter

Garnish: fresh coriander

In a large saucepan combine zests, coriander sprigs, gingerroot, peppercorns, salt, and water. Bring mixture to a boil and simmer, covered, 15 minutes. Cool mixture and strain through a sieve into a saucepan. Add shrimp and scallops and bring just to a simmer, stirring. Poach seafood until just cooked through and drain. In a bowl combine juices and add seafood. Marinate seafood, chilled and covered loosely, stirring occasionally, 3 hours.

Using a zester or fine side of a grater remove zest from 3 oranges, keeping it in long shreds, and wrap in a dampened paper towel. With a serrated knife cut away pith from same 3 oranges and cut away zest and pith from remaining 2 oranges. Cut all oranges crosswise into thin slices and chill, covered.

Make Maltaise mayonnaise:
In a bowl whisk together mayonnaise ingredients with salt and pepper to taste until smooth.

Drain seafood, discarding marinade, and in a bowl combine with bell pepper, onion or scallion, minced coriander, and zest. Add mayonnaise and toss gently to coat.

Arrange salad and orange slices on a platter lined with lettuce and garnish with coriander. Serves 6.

Photo opposite

Marinated Seafood and Blood Orange Salad

Risotto with Roasted Peppers and Onion

    6 cups low-salt chicken broth
    2 cups coarsely chopped onion
    3 tablespoons unsalted butter
    2 garlic cloves, minced
1 1/2 cups Arborio rice*
  1/3 cup dry white wine
    3 large red bell peppers, roasted
       (procedure follows) and chopped
    1 cup freshly grated Parmesan cheese

Garnish: **chopped fresh parsley leaves**

***available at specialty foods shops
and some supermarkets**

In a saucepan bring broth to a simmer and keep at a bare simmer. In a heavy 3-quart saucepan cook onion in butter over moderate heat, stirring, until softened. Add garlic and cook, stirring, until vegetables are pale golden. Stir in rice and cook over moderately low heat, stirring with a wooden spatula, until coated well with butter. Add wine and cook over moderately high heat, stirring, until absorbed. Add about ½ cup simmering broth and cook, stirring, until absorbed. Continue cooking and adding broth, about ½ cup at a time, stirring constantly and letting each portion be absorbed before adding the next, until rice is barely *al dente*. Stir in roasted peppers and more broth, about ½ cup at a time, stirring constantly and letting each portion be absorbed before adding the next, until rice is tender but still *al dente*. Remove pan from heat and immediately stir in Parmesan.

Serve *risotto* garnished with parsley. Serves 6.

To Roast Peppers

Using a long-handled fork char peppers over an open flame or on a rack set over an electric burner, turning, until skins are blackened, 4 to 6 minutes. (Or broil peppers on rack of a broiler pan under a preheated broiler about 2 inches from heat, turning every 5 minutes, 15 to 20 minutes, or until skins are blistered and charred.) Transfer peppers to a bowl and let stand, covered, until cool enough to handle. Keeping peppers whole, peel them, starting at blossom end. Cut off pepper tops and discard seeds and ribs.

Linguine with Asparagus Ricotta Sauce

2 pounds *linguine*
2 garlic cloves, minced
1 medium onion, chopped
3 tablespoons olive oil
2 tablespoons unsalted butter
1 1/2 pounds asparagus, trimmed and sliced diagonally into 1/4-inch pieces
1/4 cup dry white wine
3 tablespoons lemon juice, or to taste
2 cups ricotta cheese
1 1/2 cups half-and-half
3/4 cup freshly grated Parmesan cheese, or to taste
1/2 cup minced fresh parsley leaves

Bring a large kettle of salted water to a boil for *linguine.*

In a large stainless-steel or enameled skillet cook garlic and onion in oil and butter over moderate heat, stirring, until pale golden. Add asparagus, wine, and lemon juice and cook, stirring, 5 minutes, or until asparagus is just tender. Add ricotta, half-and-half, and salt and pepper to taste and cook over moderately low heat, stirring, until heated through.

In boiling water cook *linguine* until *al dente.* Reserve ½ cup cooking water and drain *linguine.* In a serving bowl toss pasta with ricotta sauce, Parmesan, parsley, and enough reserved cooking water to reach desired consistency. Serves 6.

Spaghetti with Chicken and Sausage Tomato Sauce

1 pound sweet Italian sausage, casings discarded
4 garlic cloves, chopped
1 1/2 cups chopped onion
1/4 cup olive oil
1 6-ounce can tomato paste
1 cup dry red wine
1 teaspoon dried thyme, crumbled
2 teaspoons dried oregano, crumbled
2 teaspoons dried basil, crumbled
3 28-ounce cans whole tomatoes including juice, chopped
2 tablespoons sugar
1 3- to 3 1/2-pound chicken, cut into serving pieces, excluding back and wings, and skinned
2 pounds spaghetti

In a heavy kettle cook sausage over moderate heat, breaking up lumps, until meat is no longer pink. Transfer sausage with a slotted spoon to paper towels to drain and pour off any fat in kettle. In kettle cook garlic and onion in oil over moderately low heat, stirring, until garlic begins to turn golden. Stir in tomato paste, wine, sausage, dried herbs, tomatoes with juice, sugar, and salt and pepper to taste. Bring mixture to a boil and simmer gently, uncovered, stirring occasionally, 2 hours. Add chicken pieces to sauce and simmer 1 hour.

Bring a kettle of salted water to a boil for spaghetti.

Transfer chicken with tongs to a cutting board and remove meat, discarding bones. Cut chicken into bite-size pieces and return to sauce. *Sauce may be made ahead and cooled completely before chilling, covered, 2 days or frozen, 1 week. Reheat sauce, thinning with water if necessary to reach desired consistency.*

In boiling water cook spaghetti until *al dente.* Drain spaghetti and in a large serving bowl toss with sauce. Serves 6 to 8.

Tomato Phyllo Pizza

14   17- by 12-inch sheets *phyllo*, stacked
     between 2 sheets of wax paper and covered
     with a dampened kitchen towel

 1   stick (1/2 cup) unsalted butter,
     melted and kept warm

14   tablespoons freshly grated Parmesan cheese
     (about 3 ounces)

 2   cups coarsely grated mozzarella cheese
     (about 1/2 pound)

 2   cups very thinly sliced onion

 4   pounds vine-ripened tomatoes (about 8), cut
     into 1/4-inch-thick slices

 1   teaspoon dried oregano, crumbled

 2   teaspoons fresh thyme leaves or
     1/2 teaspoon dried, crumbled

Garnish: thyme sprigs

Preheat oven to 375° F. and lightly butter
2 baking sheets.

On 1 prepared baking sheet arrange
1 *phyllo* sheet and brush lightly with some butter.
Sprinkle *phyllo* with 1 tablespoon Parmesan and
arrange another *phyllo* sheet on top, pressing

firmly so that it adheres to bottom layer. Butter,
sprinkle, and layer 5 more *phyllo* sheets in same
manner, ending with *phyllo*. Sprinkle top *phyllo*
sheet with half of mozzarella and scatter half
of onion evenly on top. Arrange half of tomatoes
in one layer over onion. Sprinkle pizza with
1 tablespoon Parmesan, half of oregano, half of
thyme, and salt and pepper to taste. Make another
pizza in same manner with remaining ingredients.

Bake pizzas in middle and lower third of
oven 30 to 35 minutes, or until edges are golden,
switching position of sheets in oven halfway
through baking. Arrange thyme sprigs along
edges of pizzas and with a pizza wheel or sharp
knife cut each pizza into 6 squares. Serves 6.

Photo on page 136

Turkey Chipotle Chili

2 whole canned *chipotle* chilies in *adobo**
   or 2 whole dried *chipotle* chilies**

1 cup water, boiling-hot if using dried chilies

2 pounds fresh *tomatillos*** or three 18-ounce
   cans whole *tomatillos**, drained

2 large onions, chopped

8 garlic cloves

3 tablespoons vegetable oil

2 tablespoons ground cumin

4 pounds ground turkey

2 cups chicken broth

1 bay leaf

1 1/2 teaspoons dried oregano, crumbled

2 teaspoons salt, or to taste

1 green bell pepper, chopped

2 4-ounce cans mild green chilies,
   drained and chopped

1 tablespoon cornmeal

1 19-ounce can white beans (about 2 cups),
   rinsed and drained

1/2 cup chopped fresh coriander

Accompaniment: sour cream

*available at Hispanic markets, some supermarkets, and by mail order from Adriana's Caravan, Brooklyn, NY, tel. (800) 316-0820

**available at Hispanic markets and some supermarkets

If using canned *chipotles*, in a blender purée them with water and reserve purée. If using dried *chipotles*, stem and seed them (wear rubber gloves) and in a small bowl soak them in boiling-hot water 20 minutes; in a blender purée mixture and transfer to a small bowl. If using fresh *tomatillos*, discard papery husks and wash *tomatillos* well; blanch fresh *tomatillos* in boiling water to cover 5 minutes and drain. In blender purée blanched or canned *tomatillos*.

In a large heavy kettle cook onions and 6 garlic cloves, minced, in oil over moderate heat, stirring, until onions are softened. Add cumin and cook, stirring, 30 seconds. Add turkey and cook, stirring and breaking up lumps, until meat is no longer pink. Add *chipotle* purée, *tomatillo* purée, broth, bay leaf, oregano, and salt and simmer, uncovered, adding more water if necessary to keep turkey barely covered, 1 hour. Stir in bell pepper, green chilies, and cornmeal and simmer, stirring occasionally, 30 minutes. Add white beans, fresh coriander, remaining 2 garlic cloves, minced, and salt to taste and simmer, stirring occasionally, 3 minutes, or until heated through. Discard bay leaf. *Chili may be made ahead and cooled, uncovered, before chilling, covered, 3 days or frozen, 1 week.*

Serve chili with sour cream. Makes about 14 cups, serving 6 to 8.

Photo on page 153

Red Pork and Bean Chili

6 ounces dried New Mexican red chilies*
   (about 30), stemmed and seeded
   (wear rubber gloves)

7 cups water

2 large onions, chopped

8 garlic cloves, minced

3 tablespoons vegetable oil

1 tablespoon ground cumin

4 1/2 pounds boneless pork shoulder, trimmed
   and cut into 1/2-inch pieces

1 28-ounce can whole tomatoes,
   drained and chopped

1 bay leaf

2 teaspoons salt

1 teaspoon dried oregano,
   or to taste, crumbled

1 19-ounce can (about 2 cups) kidney beans,
   rinsed and drained

Accompaniment: sour cream

*available at some specialty foods shops
and by mail order from Los Chileros de
Nueva Mexico, Santa Fe, NM, tel.
(505) 471-6967 or Adriana's Caravan,
Brooklyn, NY, tel. (800) 316-0820

In a large saucepan simmer chilies in 6 cups water
20 minutes. In a blender purée chilies with cooking liquid in batches and force purée through a
fine sieve into a bowl, pressing hard on solids.

In a large heavy kettle cook onions and
garlic in oil over moderate heat, stirring, until
onion is softened. Add cumin and cook, stirring,
30 seconds. Add pork, chili purée, tomatoes, bay
leaf, salt, oregano, and remaining 1 cup water
and simmer, uncovered, adding more water if
necessary to keep pork barely covered, 2 hours,
or until pork is tender. Add beans and simmer,
stirring occasionally, 5 minutes, or until heated
through. Discard bay leaf. *Chili may be made ahead
and cooled, uncovered, before chilling, covered, 4 days or
frozen, 1 week.*

Serve chili with sour cream. Makes about
12 cups, serving 6 to 8.

Photo opposite

New Mexican Pork and Green Chili Stew

2 medium onions, chopped

8 garlic cloves

3 tablespoons vegetable oil

4 1/2 pounds boneless pork shoulder, trimmed
   and cut into 1-inch pieces

5 pounds frozen roasted New Mexican
   green chilies*, thawed, peeled if necessary,
   seeded, and chopped (wear rubber gloves)

7 cups water

2 teaspoons salt

1 1/2 pounds boiling potatoes

*available at Hispanic markets, some
specialty foods shops, and by mail order
from Los Chileros de Nueva Mexico,
Santa Fe, NM, tel. (505) 471-6967

In a large heavy kettle cook onions and 6 garlic
cloves, minced, in oil over moderate heat, stirring,
until onions are softened. Add pork, chilies, water,
and salt and simmer, uncovered, adding more
water if necessary to keep pork barely covered, 1½
hours. Peel potatoes and cut into 1-inch pieces.
Add potatoes to stew, making sure they are covered by cooking liquid, and simmer, stirring
occasionally, 30 minutes, or until pork and
potatoes are tender. Stir in remaining 2 garlic
cloves, minced, and salt to taste and simmer 5
minutes. *Stew may be made ahead and cooled, uncovered, before chilling, covered, 3 days or frozen, 1 week.*
Makes about 14 cups, serving 6 to 8.

Photo opposite

Clockwise from bottom: Red Pork and Bean Chili;
Turkey Chipotle Chili; New Mexican Pork and Green Chili
Stew; and Black Bean Ancho Chili (pages 151 to 154)

Black Bean Ancho Chili

1 pound dried black beans (about 2 1/2 cups), picked over and rinsed
2 medium onions, chopped
6 garlic cloves
3 tablespoons vegetable oil
1 tablespoon ground cumin
7 1/2 cups water
3 ounces dried *ancho* chilies* (about 6), stemmed, seeded, and torn into pieces (wear rubber gloves)
1 28-ounce can tomatoes including juice, puréed coarse
1 cup chicken broth
1 red bell pepper, chopped
1 teaspoon dried oregano, crumbled
1/3 cup chopped fresh coriander, or to taste
2 tablespoons fresh lime juice, or to taste

Accompaniments
avocado *salsa* (recipe follows)
sour cream

*available at Hispanic markets, some specialty foods shops and supermarkets, and by mail order from Los Chileros de Nueva Mexico, Santa Fe, NM, tel. (505) 471-6967 or Adriana's Caravan, Brooklyn, NY, tel. (800) 316-0820

In a large bowl soak beans in water to cover by 2 inches 1 hour and drain. In a large heavy kettle cook onions and 4 garlic cloves, minced, in oil over moderate heat, stirring, until onions are softened. Add cumin and cook, stirring, 30 seconds. Add beans and 6 cups water and simmer, uncovered, adding more water if necessary to keep beans barely covered, 1 hour, or until beans are tender.

While beans are simmering, in a small saucepan bring remaining 1½ cups water to a boil. Add chilies and remove pan from heat. Let mixture stand 20 minutes and in a blender purée chilies with liquid. Add purée to beans with tomato purée, broth, bell pepper, oregano, and salt to taste and simmer, uncovered, stirring occasionally, 30 minutes. Stir in coriander, lime juice, and remaining 2 garlic cloves, minced, and simmer 5 minutes. *Chili may be made ahead and cooled, uncovered, before chilling, covered, 4 days or frozen, 1 week.*

Serve chili with avocado *salsa* and sour cream. Makes about 10 cups, serving 6.

Photo on page 153

◯ Avocado Salsa

1 avocado (preferably California)
1 1/2 tablespoons fresh lime juice, or to taste
1/2 cup finely chopped red onion
1 fresh or pickled *jalapeño* chili, seeded and minced (wear rubber gloves)

Halve and peel avocado and cut into ¼-inch dice. In a bowl toss avocado with remaining ingredients and salt and pepper to taste. Makes 1½ cups.

Turkey Gumbo

- 2   1-pound turkey wings
- 2   1 1/2-pound turkey drumsticks
- 1   leek, halved lengthwise and washed well
- 1   celery rib plus 1 cup chopped celery
- 1   carrot, halved
- 1   onion stuck with 2 cloves plus
      1 cup chopped onion
- 1   bay leaf
- 6   parsley stems
      a pinch of dried thyme
- 4   teaspoons salt
- 6   whole black peppercorns
- 1/4 cup lard
- 2   green bell peppers, chopped
- 1/4 cup all-purpose flour
- 1   35-ounce can whole tomatoes including
      juice, puréed through fine disk of a food mill
- 1   10-ounce package frozen corn, thawed
- 1   10-ounce package frozen okra, thawed
      and cut into 1/2-inch pieces
- 1/2 cup long-grain rice
- 2   tablespoons Worcestershire sauce
- 1/2 teaspoon cayenne, or to taste
- 1   tablespoon *filé* powder*, or to taste

Garnish: 2 tablespoons minced fresh
parsley leaves

*available at specialty foods shops

In a kettle boil turkey parts in water to cover over moderately high heat, skimming froth, 10 minutes. Add leek, celery rib, carrot, whole onion, bay leaf, parsley stems, thyme, 2 teaspoons salt, and peppercorns and simmer, covered partially, adding water as necessary to keep ingredients covered, 2½ to 3 hours, or until turkey is very tender.

Transfer turkey to a cutting board. Remove meat from bones, discarding skin, and cut into 1-inch pieces. Strain stock through a fine sieve lined with a double thickness of rinsed and squeezed cheesecloth into a large bowl and cool. *Turkey meat and stock may be made 2 days ahead and chilled, covered, separately.*

In a stainless-steel or enameled kettle melt lard over moderate heat and cook remaining 1 cup chopped onion, bell peppers, and remaining 1 cup chopped celery, stirring, 5 minutes. Stir in flour and cook over moderately low heat, stirring, 3 minutes. Add stock in a stream, stirring. Add tomato purée and bring to a boil. Add corn, okra, rice, and remaining 2 teaspoons salt and simmer 25 minutes. Add turkey meat, Worcestershire sauce, and cayenne and cook over moderately low heat until heated through.

Stir in *filé* powder and garnish with minced parsley. Serves 8 to 10.

Veal Stew

1 1/2   pounds boneless breast of veal, trimmed and cut into 2-inch pieces

1 1/2   pounds boneless veal shoulder, trimmed and cut into 2-inch pieces

3/4   cup dry white wine

1   onion, halved and each half stuck with 1 whole clove

2   carrots, each cut into 4 pieces

2   garlic cloves

    a cheesecloth bag containing 1 bay leaf, 1/2 teaspoon dried thyme, and 6 fresh parsley sprigs

4   whole black peppercorns

1/2   teaspoon salt

2   tablespoons unsalted butter

1   tablespoon vegetable oil

1   cup chopped fresh parsley leaves

3   large egg yolks

2   tablespoons *crème fraîche**

1 1/2   tablespoons fresh lemon juice, or to taste

Accompaniments
steamed rice (page 169)
French bread

*available at specialty foods shops and some supermarkets

In a heavy kettle combine veal and water to just cover it. Add wine, onion, carrots, 1 garlic clove, cheesecloth bag, peppercorns, and salt and bring to a boil, skimming froth. Simmer mixture, uncovered, skimming froth, 45 minutes. Transfer veal with a slotted spoon to a bowl. Strain veal stock through a fine sieve into another bowl, discarding cheesecloth bag, and skim fat. In cleaned kettle cook veal in butter and oil over moderate heat, stirring, 3 minutes, being careful not to brown. Add stock and simmer, uncovered, 45 minutes, or until veal is tender.

While veal is simmering, mince remaining garlic clove with parsley. Transfer veal with a slotted spoon to a heated shallow serving dish and keep warm, covered with foil. Measure stock and if necessary boil until reduced to about 1⅓ cups. In a heatproof bowl whisk yolks with *crème fraîche* and add about ⅔ cup hot stock in a stream, whisking. Add yolk mixture to remaining stock in a stream, whisking. Add lemon juice and salt and pepper to taste and cook sauce over moderately low heat, stirring constantly with a wooden spoon, until thickened slightly and registers 175° F. on a candy thermometer.

Pour sauce over veal and sprinkle stew with parsley mixture. Serve stew with rice and bread. Serves 6.

Photo opposite

more side dishes

Mixed Greens with Grapefruit, Fennel, and Parmesan (page 162)

Roasted Beets with Greens and Ginger Dressing

about 3 1/2 pounds beets including greens
For dressing
2 teaspoons coarsely grated peeled fresh gingerroot
1 tablespoon soy sauce
2 tablespoons white-wine vinegar
2 tablespoons sliced scallion
1 teaspoon sugar
1/3 cup vegetable oil

1 tablespoon unsalted butter

Garnish: 1 tablespoon minced fresh parsley leaves or coriander

Preheat oven to 350° F.

Cut greens from beets, leaving about 1 inch of stems attached, and reserve greens. Scrub beets and wrap tightly in 2 foil packages. Roast beets on a baking sheet in middle of oven 1 to 1½ hours, or until tender.

Make dressing:

In a blender blend together all dressing ingredients except oil. With motor running add oil in a stream, blending until emulsified.

Unwrap beets carefully, discarding any liquid, and cool until they can be handled. Peel and halve beets. Cut beets into ¼-inch-thick slices and in a bowl toss with dressing and salt and pepper to taste.

Wash reserved greens well and drain. In a large skillet sauté greens with salt and pepper to taste in butter over moderately high heat, stirring, until wilted, 3 to 4 minutes. Transfer greens to a platter and spoon beets and dressing over them.

Garnish beets with parsley or coriander and serve at room temperature. Serves 6.

Honey-Glazed Carrots

1 1/2 pounds carrots, cut into 1-inch pieces
1/3 cup fresh orange juice
1/4 cup honey
2 tablespoons unsalted butter
1/2 teaspoon freshly grated orange zest
1/4 teaspoon ground ginger

In a heavy saucepan of boiling salted water simmer carrots until just tender, about 10 minutes, and drain.

In pan bring remaining ingredients to a boil, stirring occasionally, and boil until reduced to about ¼ cup. Add carrots and cook, shaking pan, until most liquid is evaporated and carrots are evenly glazed. Serves 6.

Sweet and Savory Escarole

4 garlic cloves
3 tablespoons olive oil
3 heads escarole (about 2 1/2 pounds), rinsed and torn into bite-size pieces
1/2 cup chicken broth
1/4 cup oil-cured olives, pitted and chopped
1/4 cup raisins
2 tablespoons capers, lightly crushed

Garnish: 1 tablespoon pine nuts, lightly toasted and chopped

In a large heavy kettle cook garlic in oil over moderate heat just until it begins to turn golden and discard. Add half of escarole and cook over high heat, stirring, until it begins to wilt. Add remaining escarole and cook, stirring, until it wilts and most liquid is evaporated. Add remaining ingredients and simmer, stirring, 15 minutes. Season mixture with salt and pepper to taste.

Garnish escarole with toasted pine nuts. Serves 6 to 8.

Onion and Potato Gratin

    4   cups thinly sliced onions (about 4)
    3   tablespoons unsalted butter
    1   pound russet (baking) potatoes (about 2)
    1   cup heavy cream
    1/4 cup freshly grated Parmesan cheese
    1/4 cup grated Gruyère cheese

Preheat oven to 400° F. and butter a 2-quart gratin dish.

In a large skillet cook onions with salt and pepper to taste in butter over moderate heat, stirring occasionally, 15 minutes, or until golden. Peel potatoes and cut into ⅛-inch-thick slices. Spoon half of onions into prepared dish and cover with potato slices. Season potatoes with salt and pepper to taste and cover with remaining onions. Pour cream over mixture and sprinkle top with cheeses. Bake gratin in middle of oven 30 to 40 minutes, or until potatoes are tender and top is golden brown. Serves 6.

Cherry Tomatoes and Green Beans

    1   pound green beans, trimmed and cut
        diagonally into 1-inch pieces
    1   pint vine-ripened cherry tomatoes,
        picked over
    1   teaspoon minced garlic
    2   tablespoons vegetable oil
    3/4 teaspoon minced fresh rosemary leaves
        or 1/4 teaspoon dried, crumbled

In a saucepan of boiling salted water cook beans 4 minutes, or until crisp-tender, and drain in a colander. Rinse beans under cold water to stop cooking and pat dry. In a stainless-steel or enameled skillet sauté tomatoes and garlic in oil over moderately high heat, stirring, 1 minute, or until tomatoes just begin to blister. Add beans and rosemary and sauté, stirring, until heated through. Season mixture with salt and pepper to taste. Serves 6.

Baked Sweet Potatoes with Spiced Apple and Prunes

    3   pounds sweet potatoes
    1   Granny Smith apple, peeled, cored,
        halved lengthwise, and sliced thin
    3/4 stick (6 tablespoons) unsalted butter
    1   teaspoon cinnamon
    1/4 teaspoon ground cloves
    1/2 cup minced pitted prunes or raisins
    1/4 cup firmly packed light brown sugar
    1/4 cup coarse dry bread crumbs

Preheat oven to 375° F. and butter a 1½-quart gratin dish.

In a large saucepan combine potatoes with water to cover and bring to a boil. Simmer potatoes, covered, 25 to 30 minutes, or until just tender, and drain. Cool potatoes until they can be handled. Peel potatoes and cut crosswise into ½-inch-thick slices.

Arrange potatoes, overlapping slightly, in one layer in prepared dish. In a skillet cook apple in 3 tablespoons butter over moderate heat, stirring, 3 minutes, or until softened, and stir in cinnamon, cloves, prunes or raisins, and sugar, stirring to coat apple well. In a small saucepan melt remaining 3 tablespoons butter and stir in bread crumbs. Layer apple mixture evenly over potatoes and sprinkle with bread crumbs. Bake potato mixture in middle of oven 20 minutes. Serves 6 to 8.

Mixed Greens with Grapefruit, Fennel, and Parmesan

For dressing
- 1   small garlic clove, minced and mashed to a paste with 1/4 teaspoon salt
- 3   tablespoons fresh grapefruit juice
- 3   tablespoons white-wine vinegar
- 1 1/2   teaspoons Dijon mustard
- 1/2   cup olive oil
- 1/3   cup minced fresh parsley leaves (preferably flat-leafed)

- 8   cups coarsely shredded romaine
- 3   cups *arugula* or watercress, coarse stems discarded and leaves washed well and spun dry
- 3   cups thinly sliced fennel (sometimes called anise)
- 1   cup thinly sliced radishes
- 3   ounces Parmesan cheese, shaved into curls with a vegetable peeler (about 1 1/2 cups)
- 3   large grapefruit, zest and pith cut away with a serrated knife and fruit cut into sections

Make dressing:

In a small bowl whisk together garlic paste, grapefruit juice, vinegar, and mustard. Add oil in a stream, whisking until emulsified. *Dressing may be prepared up to this point 1 day ahead and chilled, covered.* Whisk in parsley and salt and pepper to taste.

In a large bowl toss together romaine, *arugula* or watercress, fennel, radishes, and dressing. Add Parmesan and grapefruit sections, cut into 1-inch pieces, and toss gently. Serves 6.

Photo on page 158

Mixed Lettuces with Herb Vinaigrette

For vinaigrette
- 2   tablespoons white-wine vinegar
- 1   teaspoon Dijon mustard
- 1/4   teaspoon dried thyme, crumbled
- 1/4   teaspoon sugar
- 1   small shallot, minced
- 1/3   cup olive oil

- 8   cups mixed lettuces, washed and spun dry

Make vinaigrette:

In a small bowl whisk together all vinaigrette ingredients except oil with salt to taste. Add oil in a stream, whisking until emulsified.

In a large salad bowl toss lettuces with vinaigrette and pepper to taste. Serves 6.

Red Cabbage and Apple Slaw with Blue Cheese Dressing

2 Granny Smith apples, peeled and cut into 1/4-inch cubes
2 tablespoons fresh lemon juice
1 head red cabbage (about 2 pounds), thinly sliced
1/3 cup finely chopped scallion
   For dressing
1/4 pound blue cheese, crumbled
1/2 cup sour cream
1/2 cup mayonnaise
1 tablespoon white-wine vinegar
1/3 cup vegetable oil
   pinch of cayenne

Garnish: 3 tablespoons finely chopped fresh parsley leaves

In a salad bowl toss apples with lemon juice. Add cabbage and scallion and combine well.

Make dressing:

In a food processor or blender blend blue cheese, sour cream, mayonnaise, and vinegar until smooth. With motor running add oil in a stream with cayenne and salt and pepper to taste, blending until emulsified.

Toss slaw with dressing and garnish with parsley. Serves 6 to 8.

Chick-Pea Vegetable Salad

For vinaigrette
3 tablespoons Sherry vinegar or red-wine vinegar
3 tablespoons fresh lemon juice
1/3 cup olive oil

4 cups cooked dried chick-peas or two 20-ounce cans, drained
1 vine-ripened tomato, seeded and minced
1 green bell pepper, minced
2 celery ribs, minced
3/4 cup chopped cooked green beans
3 scallions, minced
   soft-leafed lettuce leaves for lining platter

Garnish: minced fresh parsley leaves and pimiento strips

Make vinaigrette:

In a ceramic or glass bowl stir together vinegar, lemon juice, and salt and pepper to taste and add oil in a stream, whisking until emulsified.

In a small saucepan heat chick-peas in about 2 cups water over moderately low heat until heated through and drain. Add chick-peas to vinaigrette and cool. Add remaining ingredients except lettuce with salt and pepper to taste and toss well. Line a platter with lettuce and mound salad in center.

Serve salad garnished with parsley and pimiento. Serves 6 to 8.

Minted Pea and New Potato Salad

1 1/2   pounds small new potatoes
  1/3   cup white-wine vinegar
1 1/2   tablespoons vegetable oil
    3   cups shelled fresh peas (about 2 pounds
        unshelled) or thawed frozen peas, drained
  1/2   cup mayonnaise
  1/4   cup finely chopped fresh mint leaves

In a saucepan combine potatoes with salted water to cover by 2 inches and simmer, covered partially, until just tender, 12 to 15 minutes. Drain potatoes and cool just until they can be handled. Quarter potatoes and halve quarters. In a bowl drizzle warm potatoes with vinegar and oil and season with salt and pepper to taste. Toss potatoes to coat. *Marinate potatoes, covered and chilled, at least 2 hours or overnight.*

In a saucepan boil peas in 2 quarts salted water until tender, 3 to 5 minutes, and drain. To potatoes add peas, mayonnaise, mint, and salt and pepper to taste and stir together gently.

Serve pea and potato salad at room temperature. Serves 6.

Tomato and Mozzarella Salad with Balsamic Basil Vinaigrette

For vinaigrette
  3   tablespoons balsamic vinegar
  1   teaspoon chopped garlic
1/4   cup olive oil (preferably extra-virgin)
1/3   cup chopped fresh basil leaves

2 1/2   pounds vine-ripened tomatoes (about
        6 medium), cut into 1/2-inch-thick slices
    1   pound fresh mozzarella cheese, sliced thin
  1/2   cup thinly sliced sweet onion such as
        Vidalia, separated into rings

Garnish: basil sprigs

Make vinaigrette:
In a blender blend together vinegar, garlic, and salt and pepper to taste. With motor running add oil in a stream, blending until emulsified. Stir in basil.

Arrange tomato slices alternately with mozzarella slices on a deep platter and scatter onion on top. *Salad may be prepared up to this point 4 hours ahead and chilled, covered.* Pour vinaigrette over salad and let stand 20 minutes.

Garnish salad with basil. Serves 6 to 8.

Green Bean, Red Onion, and Roasted Potato Salad with Rosemary Vinaigrette

3 pounds red boiling potatoes
1/3 cup olive oil
For vinaigrette
1 garlic clove
1/4 cup red-wine vinegar
1 tablespoon fresh rosemary leaves or 1 teaspoon dried, crumbled
1/3 cup olive oil

1 red onion, halved lengthwise and sliced thin lengthwise
2 pounds green beans, trimmed and cut into 1-inch pieces
about 24 Kalamata or Niçoise olives, pitted and halved

Garnish: rosemary sprigs

Preheat oven to 425° F.

Halve red boiling potatoes, unpeeled, and cut into 1-inch wedges. In a large roasting pan heat olive oil in middle of oven 5 minutes. Add potatoes, tossing to coat, and roast, stirring every 10 minutes, for 30 minutes, or until tender. Cool potatoes in pan.

Make vinaigrette:

In a blender purée all vinaigrette ingredients except olive oil with salt to taste. With motor running add olive oil in a stream, blending until emulsified.

In a small bowl of ice and cold water soak onion 5 minutes. Drain onion well and pat dry. In a kettle of boiling salted water cook beans 4 minutes, or until crisp-tender, and drain in a colander. Rinse beans under cold water to stop cooking and pat dry. In a very large bowl combine potatoes, onion, beans, and olives. Add vinaigrette and toss gently.

Serve salad garnished with rosemary. Serves 8 to 10.

Photo on page 167

⊙+ Antipasto Pasta Salad

1 pound *rotini* or *fusilli* (spiral pastas)
For dressing
2 garlic cloves
1 tablespoon Dijon mustard
1/3 cup red-wine vinegar
2 tablespoons balsamic vinegar
1 tablespoon water
1/2 cup vegetable oil

1 ounce sun-dried tomatoes (not packed in oil, about 1/2 cup), soaked in hot water 5 minutes and drained well
1/2 pound smoked mozzarella cheese, cut into 1/2-inch cubes
1 1-pound can chick-peas, drained and rinsed
3 1/2 ounces sliced hard salami, cut into julienne strips
10 to 20 bottled small *peperoncini* (pickled Tuscan peppers)
1/2 teaspoon dried hot red pepper flakes
1 cup loosely packed fresh flat-leafed parsley leaves, minced

In a kettle of boiling salted water cook pasta until *al dente* and drain in a colander. Rinse pasta under cold water and drain well.

Make dressing:

In a blender blend all dressing ingredients except oil with salt to taste. With motor running add vegetable oil in a stream, blending until emulsified.

In a very large bowl toss pasta well with dressing and stir in remaining ingredients. *Chill pasta salad, covered, at least 1 hour and up to 2 days.* Serves 8 to 10.

Photo on page 167

Curried Rice Salad with Melon, Raisins, and Peanuts

2 cups long-grain rice
1 1/2 teaspoons salt
2 1/2 teaspoons curry powder
3 tablespoons white-wine vinegar
1/3 cup vegetable oil
3/4 cup golden raisins
1 cantaloupe, seeded and cut into 1/2-inch cubes
1 cup plain yogurt
1/4 cup Major Grey's chutney

Garnish: 1/3 cup unsalted roasted peanuts

In a large saucepan bring 4 quarts water to a boil. Stir in rice and salt, stirring until water returns to a boil, and boil 10 minutes. Drain rice in a large sieve and rinse. Set sieve over a large saucepan of simmering water and steam rice, covered with a folded kitchen towel and lid, 15 minutes, or until fluffy and dry. Transfer rice to a very large bowl and cool to lukewarm.

In a small bowl whisk together 1½ teaspoons curry powder, vinegar, oil, and salt to taste and add to rice, tossing well. Stir in raisins and cantaloupe. In a blender blend yogurt, chutney, and remaining teaspoon curry powder until dressing is smooth. Pour dressing over rice salad and toss well. *Chill salad, covered, at least 1 hour and up to 2 days.*

Serve rice salad garnished with peanuts. Serves 10 to 12.

Photo opposite

☺+ Couscous Tabbouleh

1 cup chicken broth
1 cup water
1/2 cup fresh lemon juice
1/3 cup plus 2 tablespoons olive oil
1 1/2 cups couscous
1 seedless cucumber, cut into 1/4-inch pieces
8 vine-ripened plum tomatoes, seeded and cut into 1/4-inch pieces
3/4 cup finely chopped scallion
2 cups loosely packed fresh parsley leaves, minced
1 cup loosely packed fresh mint leaves, minced

Garnish: mint sprigs, cucumber slices, and tomato slices

In a saucepan bring broth, water, ¼ cup lemon juice, and 2 tablespoons oil to a boil and stir in couscous. Remove pan from heat and let couscous stand, covered, 5 minutes. Fluff couscous with a fork and cool in pan.

In a very large bowl stir together cucumber, plum tomatoes, scallion, remaining ⅓ cup oil, remaining ¼ cup lemon juice, and salt to taste and let stand 15 minutes. Stir in couscous, parsley, and mint. *Chill salad, covered, at least 1 hour and up to 2 days.*

Serve salad garnished with mint sprigs, cucumber slices, and tomato slices. Serves 8 to 10.

Photo opposite

Clockwise from upper right: Green Bean, Red Onion, and Roasted Potato Salad with Rosemary Vinaigrette; Couscous Tabbouleh; Antipasto Pasta Salad; and Curried Rice Salad with Melon, Raisins, and Peanuts (pages 165 to 166)

◔ Saffron Couscous

3/4 teaspoon saffron threads, crumbled
2 1/4 cups water
3 tablespoons unsalted butter
1 teaspoon salt
1 10-ounce box couscous (about 1 1/2 cups)
1 garlic clove, minced
2 teaspoons fresh lemon juice, or to taste
1/4 cup minced fresh chives

Set a rack over a saucepan of boiling water. Put saffron in a heatproof saucer on rack and steam, covered, 3 minutes, or until brittle.

In a saucepan bring 2¼ cups water to a boil with butter and salt and stir in couscous, brittle saffron, crumbled fine, garlic, and lemon juice. Remove pan from heat and let couscous stand, covered, 5 minutes. Stir in chives and pepper to taste. Serves 6.

◑+ Dilled Mushroom Barley Pilaf

1 small onion, minced
2 tablespoons unsalted butter
1 tablespoon vegetable oil
1/2 pound mushrooms, sliced
1 1/2 cups pearl barley
2 cups beef broth
1 cup water
1/2 teaspoon freshly ground black pepper
1 tablespoon fresh lemon juice, or to taste
1 1/2 tablespoons chopped fresh dill or
1 1/4 teaspoons dried, crumbled

Preheat oven to 350° F.

In a large ovenproof saucepan cook onion in butter and oil over moderate heat, stirring, until softened. Add mushrooms and cook, stirring, 2 minutes, or until mushrooms begin to give off liquid. Add barley and cook, stirring, 2 minutes. Add broth, water, pepper, and salt to taste and bring to a boil. Bake pilaf, covered, in middle of oven 45 minutes, or until liquid is absorbed. Fluff pilaf immediately with a fork and let stand, covered, 5 minutes. Stir in lemon juice and dill. Serves 6.

Steamed Rice

1   tablespoon salt
2   cups long-grain rice

In a large saucepan bring 5 quarts water to a boil with salt. Sprinkle in rice, stirring until water returns to a boil, and boil 10 minutes. In a large colander drain rice and rinse. Set colander over a large saucepan of boiling water and steam rice, covered with a kitchen towel and lid, 15 minutes, or until fluffy and dry. Makes about 6 cups.

Lemon Brown Rice with Zucchini and Dill

2 1/3   cups chicken broth
  1/4   cup fresh lemon juice
    1   teaspoon freshly grated lemon zest
  1/2   teaspoon salt
    1   tablespoon vegetable oil
1 1/3   cups long-grain brown rice
    1   zucchini, cut into 1/4-inch slices
  1/4   cup chopped fresh dill
  1/2   stick (1/4 cup) unsalted butter, softened

In a heavy 3-quart saucepan bring broth, lemon juice, zest, salt, and oil to a boil. Stir in rice and cook, covered, over low heat 40 minutes. Stir in zucchini, dill, and salt and pepper to taste and simmer, covered, until zucchini is tender, about 10 minutes. Stir in butter and remove pan from heat. Let rice stand, covered, 3 minutes and fluff with a fork. Serves 6 to 8.

Buttered Egg Noodles with Lemon and Poppy Seeds

3/4   pound wide egg noodles
1/2   cup finely chopped shallot
1/2   cup finely chopped celery
  3   tablespoons unsalted butter
  2   tablespoons olive oil
  2   teaspoons freshly grated lemon zest
  3   tablespoons poppy seeds

Bring a kettle of salted water to a boil for noodles.

In a large deep skillet cook shallot and celery in butter and oil over moderate heat, stirring, until celery is softened. Stir in zest and poppy seeds and remove skillet from heat.

Cook noodles in boiling water until just *al dente*, about 6 minutes, and drain well. Add noodles to shallot mixture with salt and pepper to taste and toss until coated well. Serves 6.

The following stuffing recipes can be used to stuff a 12- to 14-pound turkey or can be baked separately in a 3- to 4-quart casserole or shallow baking dish; the latter option produces a slightly drier and more crisp stuffing.

Corn Bread, Sausage, and Scallion Stuffing

For corn bread

1	cup all-purpose flour
1 1/3	cups yellow cornmeal
1	tablespoon baking powder
1	teaspoon salt
1	cup milk
1	large egg
3	tablespoons unsalted butter, melted and cooled

3/4	pound bulk pork sausage
3/4	stick (6 tablespoons) unsalted butter plus an additional 2 tablespoons if baking stuffing separately
2	cups finely chopped onion
1 1/2	cups finely chopped celery
2	teaspoons dried sage, crumbled
1	teaspoon dried marjoram, crumbled
1	teaspoon dried rosemary, crumbled
1/2	cup thinly sliced scallion
1 1/2	cups chicken broth if baking stuffing separately

Make corn bread:

Preheat oven to 425° F. and butter an 8-inch square baking pan.

In a bowl stir together flour, cornmeal, baking powder, and salt. In a small bowl whisk together milk, egg, and butter and stir into cornmeal mixture until just combined. Pour batter into prepared pan and bake in middle of oven 20 to 25 minutes, or until a tester comes out clean. Cool corn bread in pan on a rack 5 minutes. Invert corn bread onto rack and cool completely. *Corn bread may be made 2 days ahead and kept wrapped tightly in foil at room temperature.*

Reduce temperature to 325° F.

Into a shallow baking pan crumble corn bread coarse and bake in middle of oven, stirring occasionally, 30 minutes, or until dry and golden. Cool corn bread completely. In a large skillet cook sausage over moderate heat, stirring occasionally, until no longer pink and transfer with a slotted spoon to a bowl. To fat in skillet add 6 tablespoons butter and cook onion and celery over moderately low heat, stirring occasionally, until softened. Add dried herbs and salt and pepper to taste and cook, stirring, 3 minutes. Transfer onion mixture to a large bowl and add corn bread, sausage, scallion, and salt and pepper to taste, combining gently but thoroughly. Cool stuffing completely before using to stuff a 12- to 14-pound turkey.

Stuffing may also be baked separately: Spoon stuffing into a buttered 3- to 4-quart casserole. Drizzle stuffing with broth and dot with additional 2 tablespoons butter, cut into bits. Bake stuffing, covered, in middle of a preheated 325° F. oven 30 minutes and bake, uncovered, 30 minutes more. Serves 8 to 10.

Photo on page 173

☺+ Raisin Bread, Cranberry, and Rosemary Stuffing

2 cups finely chopped onion

1 stick (1/2 cup) unsalted butter plus an additional 2 tablespoons if baking stuffing separately

2 cups fresh cranberries, picked over and chopped coarse

2 tablespoons firmly packed light brown sugar

2 teaspoons dried rosemary, crumbled

1/2 teaspoon dried sage, crumbled

12 slices raisin bread, cut into 1/2-inch cubes, toasted, and cooled (about 7 1/2 cups)

1/2 cup fresh orange juice

1/2 cup chicken broth if baking stuffing separately

In a large skillet cook onion in 1 stick butter over moderately low heat, stirring occasionally, until softened. Add cranberries, sugar, rosemary, sage, and salt and pepper to taste and cook, stirring, 3 minutes. Transfer mixture to a large bowl and add toasted bread cubes, orange juice, and salt and pepper to taste, combining gently but thoroughly. Cool stuffing completely before using to stuff a 12- to 14-pound turkey.

Stuffing may also be baked separately: Spoon stuffing into a buttered 3- to 4-quart casserole. Drizzle stuffing with broth and dot with additional 2 tablespoons butter, cut into bits. Bake stuffing, covered, in middle of a preheated 325° F. oven 30 minutes and bake, uncovered, 30 minutes more. Serves 8 to 10.

Photo on page 173

☺+ Green Chili Stuffing

2 cups finely chopped onion

2 cups finely chopped celery

1 stick (1/2 cup) unsalted butter plus an additional 2 tablespoons if baking stuffing separately

2 4-ounce cans chopped mild green chilies including juice

2 pickled *jalapeño* chilies, minced (about 1 tablespoon), or to taste (wear rubber gloves)

3/4 teaspoon chili powder

1/2 teaspoon dried thyme, crumbled

1/2 teaspoon dried oregano, crumbled

1 1/2 teaspoons ground cumin

1 cup finely chopped pecans, lightly toasted

1 1-pound loaf homemade-type white bread, cut into 1/2-inch cubes, toasted, and cooled

3/4 cup chicken broth if baking stuffing separately

In a large skillet cook onion and celery in 1 stick butter over moderate heat, stirring occasionally, until onion is softened and pale golden. Add green chilies with juice, *jalapeños*, chili powder, thyme, oregano, cumin, and salt and pepper to taste and cook, stirring, 3 minutes. Transfer mixture to a large bowl and add pecans, toasted bread cubes, and salt and pepper to taste, combining gently but thoroughly. Cool stuffing completely before using to stuff a 12- to 14-pound turkey.

Stuffing may also be baked separately: Spoon stuffing into a buttered 3- to 4-quart casserole. Drizzle stuffing with broth and dot with additional 2 tablespoons butter, cut into bits. Bake stuffing, covered, in middle of a preheated 325° F. oven 30 minutes and bake, uncovered, 30 minutes more. Serves 8 to 10.

Photo on page 173

Mashed Potato and Sautéed Apple Stuffing

    4 russet (baking) potatoes (about 2 pounds)
    3 cups finely chopped onion
    2 cups finely chopped celery
1 1/2 sticks (3/4 cup) unsalted butter
       plus an additional 2 tablespoons if
       baking stuffing separately
    2 Granny Smith apples (about 1 1/4 pounds)
    1 tablespoon cider vinegar
  1/2 teaspoon dried sage, crumbled
  1/2 teaspoon dried rosemary, crumbled
  1/2 teaspoon dried thyme, crumbled
  1/2 teaspoon dried marjoram, crumbled
  1/4 cup finely chopped fresh parsley leaves
  1/4 cup milk, scalded
    8 slices homemade-type white bread, cut
       into 1/4-inch cubes, toasted, and cooled
       (about 5 cups)
  1/3 cup chicken broth if baking stuffing
       separately

Peel potatoes and cut into 1-inch pieces. In a steamer set over a large pan of simmering water steam potatoes, covered, 20 to 25 minutes, or until very tender.

While potatoes are steaming, in a large skillet cook onion and celery in 1¼ sticks butter over moderately low heat, stirring occasionally, until softened. Peel apples and chop fine. Add apples to onion mixture and cook over moderate heat, stirring occasionally, until tender. Stir in vinegar and herbs and sauté over moderately high heat, stirring, 3 minutes.

Transfer warm steamed potatoes to a large bowl and mash with a potato masher. Whisk in milk, 2 tablespoons butter, cut into bits, and salt and pepper to taste until smooth.

To mashed potatoes add apple mixture, toasted bread cubes, and salt and pepper to taste and combine well. Cool stuffing completely before using to stuff a 12- to 14-pound turkey.

Stuffing may also be baked separately: Spoon stuffing into a buttered 3- to 4-quart casserole. Drizzle stuffing with broth and dot with additional 2 tablespoons butter, cut into bits. Bake stuffing, covered, in middle of a preheated 325° F. oven 30 minutes and bake, uncovered, 30 minutes more. Serves 8 to 10.

Photo opposite

Clockwise from top: Corn Bread, Sausage, and Scallion Stuffing; Green Chili Stuffing; Mashed Potato and Sautéed Apple Stuffing; and Raisin Bread, Cranberry, and Rosemary Stuffing (pages 170 to 172)

more
desserts

Blueberry Buttermilk Tart and Blueberry Ice Cream (page 185)

White Buttermilk Cake with Almond Caramel Frosting

  1   cup buttermilk
1/2   teaspoon almond extract
1/2   teaspoon vanilla
  2   sticks (1 cup) unsalted butter, softened
  2   cups sugar
  3   cups all-purpose flour
  1   teaspoon baking soda
1/2   teaspoon salt
  6   large egg whites
      a pinch cream of tartar
      almond caramel frosting (recipe follows)

Preheat oven to 375° F. Butter and flour two 9-inch round cake pans, knocking out excess.

In a small bowl stir together buttermilk, almond extract, and vanilla. In a large bowl with a wooden spoon beat together butter and sugar. Into a bowl sift together flour, baking soda, and salt and stir into butter mixture alternately with buttermilk mixture. In another bowl beat whites with a pinch salt and cream of tartar until they hold stiff peaks. Stir one fourth of whites into batter to lighten and fold in remaining whites gently but throughly.

Divide batter between prepared pans, smoothing tops, and bake in middle of oven 30 to 35 minutes, or until a tester comes out clean. Cool layers in pans on racks 10 minutes. Turn layers out onto racks and cool completely. *Cake layers may be made 2 weeks ahead and frozen, wrapped well in plastic wrap and foil. Defrost layers, wrapped, at room temperature.*

Working quickly and using a metal spatula dipped in cold water spread almond carmel frosting between layers and on top and side of cake.

○ Almond Caramel Frosting

  1   cup milk
  3   cups firmly packed light brown sugar
1/4   cup almond-flavored liqueur
  1   stick (1/2 cup) unsalted butter, cut into bits
  1   teaspoon hot water if necessary

In a large heavy saucepan bring milk, sugar, liqueur, and butter to a boil over moderate heat, stirring, and cook, without stirring, until mixture reaches soft-ball stage (238° F. on a candy thermometer). Remove saucepan from heat and cool mixture until it stops bubbling. Transfer mixture to a large heatproof bowl and with an electric mixer beat until cool and of spreading consistency. If frosting becomes too hard to spread beat in hot water.

Angel Food Cake with Chocolate Icing and Almonds

For cake
- 1 **cup cake flour (not self-rising)**
- 1 2/3 **cups sugar**
- 1 3/4 **cups egg whites (from about 13 large eggs)**
- 1/2 **teaspoon salt**
- 1 **teaspoon cream of tartar**
- 1/2 **teaspoon almond extract, or to taste**
For icing
- 1/3 **cup heavy cream**
- 3/4 **cup semisweet chocolate chips**

- 1 1/2 **cups sliced almonds, toasted**

Make cake:

Preheat oven to 300° F.

Sift flour 3 times onto a sheet of wax paper. In sifter combine sifted flour and ⅔ cup sugar and sift onto another sheet of wax paper. In a large bowl with an electric mixer beat whites until broken up. Add salt and cream of tartar and beat until frothy. Beat in remaining cup sugar, a little at a time, and almond extract and beat until whites hold soft peaks. Sift one fourth of flour mixture over whites, folding it in gently but thoroughly, and sift and fold remaining flour mixture in batches into whites in same manner. Spoon batter into a very clean, ungreased tube pan, 10 by 8¼ by 4¼ inches, preferably with a removable bottom, smoothing top, and rap pan on a hard surface twice to eliminate any air bubbles. Bake cake in middle of oven 1 hour, or until springy to the touch and a tester comes out clean. If pan has feet invert pan over work surface; otherwise invert pan over neck of a bottle. *Cool cake at least 1 hour or overnight.* Run a thin knife in a sawing motion around edge of pan and tube to loosen cake and invert cake onto a serving plate.

Make icing:

In a saucepan bring cream to a boil over moderate heat. Remove pan from heat and add chips, whisking until smooth.

Cool icing until slightly thickened and spread on top of cake, allowing excess to run down side. Sprinkle almonds on top of cake.

Espresso Cheesecake

For crust
- 2 **cups finely ground Oreo cookies (about 20)**
- 1/2 **stick (1/4 cup) unsalted butter, melted**
For filling
- 1/4 **cup coffee-flavored liqueur**
- 2 **tablespoons instant espresso powder**
- 2 **pounds cream cheese at room temperature**
- 1 1/2 **cups firmly packed dark brown sugar**
- 3 **large eggs**
- 1/2 **cup sour cream**
- 1/4 **teaspoon salt**
- 1 **teaspoon vanilla**

Preheat oven to 350° F. and wrap outside of a 9-inch springform pan with heavy-duty foil.

Make crust:

In a bowl stir together crumbs and butter until combined well and press onto bottom and halfway up side of prepared pan.

Make filling:

In a small bowl stir together liqueur and espresso powder. In a large bowl with an electric mixer beat cream cheese until smooth. Add sugar and beat until light and fluffy. Beat in eggs, 1 at a time, beating well after each addition, and beat in espresso mixture and remaining ingredients.

Pour filling into crust and bake in middle of oven 1 hour. (Cheesecake will not set until it cools.) Turn off oven and cool cheesecake completely in oven with door ajar. *Chill cheesecake covered, at least overnight and up to 2 days.*

Carrot Raisin Cake with Irish Cream Frosting

For cake
about **1 pound carrots**
2 1/2 **cups all-purpose flour**
1 1/2 **tablespoons baking powder**
1/2 **teaspoon salt**
2 **teaspoons cinnamon**
1/8 **teaspoon freshly grated nutmeg**
1/4 **teaspoon ground allspice**
1 **cup vegetable oil**
1 **cup firmly packed brown sugar**
4 **large eggs**
1/4 **cup fresh orange juice**
1/2 **cup raisins**
2 **teaspoons freshly grated orange zest**
For frosting
2 **sticks (1 cup) unsalted butter, softened**
2 1/4 **cups confectioners' sugar**
1/2 **teaspoon salt**
1/4 **cup Irish cream liqueur or heavy cream**

Garnish: **confectioners' sugar**

Make cake:

Preheat oven to 350° F. Butter and flour two 8-inch round cake pans, knocking out excess.

Using large teardrop holes of a grater coarsely shred enough carrots to measure 2½ cups. (Do not use rough side of grater.) In a bowl whisk together flour, baking powder, salt, and spices. In another bowl whisk together oil, brown sugar, and eggs until combined well and with a wooden spoon stir in flour mixture in 2 batches alternately with orange juice until combined well. Stir in carrots, raisins, and zest until just combined.

Divide batter between prepared pans, smoothing tops, and bake in middle of oven 30 to 35 minutes, or until a tester comes out clean and edges begin to pull away from sides of pans. Cool layers in pans 20 minutes. Turn layers out onto racks and cool completely. *Cake layers may be made 1 day ahead and kept, wrapped well, at room temperature or 2 weeks ahead and kept, wrapped well in plastic wrap and foil, frozen. Defrost layers, wrapped, at room temperature.*

Make frosting:

In a bowl with an electric mixer beat butter until smooth. Beat in confectioners' sugar gradually and add salt and liqueur or cream, beating until light and fluffy.

Spread some frosting between layers and decoratively on side of cake and reserve remaining frosting in a pastry bag fitted with a star tip. Put a paper doily on top of cake and sift confectioners' sugar over it. Remove doily carefully. Pipe reserved frosting decoratively around edge of cake.

Photo opposite

Carrot Raisin Cake with Irish Cream Frosting

Cherry Ice Cream Sundae Cake with Hot Fudge Sauce

1 1/2   cups dried sour cherries*
   6   tablespoons kirsch or brandy
     For cake
 3/4   cup all-purpose flour
 1/4   cup plus 2 tablespoons unsweetened
     cocoa powder (not Dutch process)
 3/4   teaspoon baking powder
 1/2   teaspoon baking soda
 1/4   teaspoon salt
 1/2   cup sour cream
   3   tablespoons water
   1   teaspoon vanilla
   1   stick (1/2 cup) unsalted butter, softened
 2/3   cup firmly packed light brown sugar
   1   large egg

   2   pints premium-quality vanilla ice cream,
     slightly softened
     For sauce
   1   ounce unsweetened chocolate, chopped
   1   tablespoon unsalted butter
   1   tablespoon light corn syrup
 1/2   cup heavy cream plus an additional
     2 tablespoons for thinning if desired
 1/2   cup granulated sugar
   1   teaspoon vanilla
   a   pinch salt

     Garnish: whipped cream and
     chopped walnuts

     *available at specialty foods shops

In a saucepan toss cherries with kirsch or brandy and simmer, covered, 5 minutes. Cool cherries.

Make cake:

Preheat oven to 350° F. Butter and flour a 9-inch square baking pan, knocking out excess.

Into a bowl sift together flour, cocoa powder, baking powder, baking soda, and salt. In a small bowl whisk together sour cream, water, and vanilla. In a large bowl with an electric mixer beat together butter and brown sugar until light and fluffy and beat in egg. Add flour mixture in batches alternately with sour cream mixture, beginning and ending with flour mixture. Pour batter into prepared pan, smoothing top, and bake in middle of oven 25 minutes, or until a tester comes out clean. Cool cake completely in pan on a rack.

In a bowl stir cherry mixture into ice cream and spread on top of cake in pan. *Freeze cherry ice cream sundae cake, wrapped well in plastic wrap, at least 2 hours, or until firm, and up to 1 week.*

Make sauce:

In a heavy saucepan heat chocolate, butter, corn syrup, cream (if a thinner sauce is desired add additional 2 tablespoons cream), and granulated sugar over moderately low heat, stirring, until sugar is dissolved and boil over moderate heat, without stirring, 5 minutes. Remove pan from heat. Stir in vanilla and salt and cool slightly.

Cut cake into squares. Serve sundae cake topped with sauce, whipped cream, and walnuts.

Peach Shortcakes

- 6 peaches, peeled and chopped
- 1 tablespoon fresh lemon juice
- 1/3 cup granulated sugar
- 1 tablespoon peach schnapps

For biscuits

- 1 1/2 cups all-purpose flour
- 1/2 cup graham cracker crumbs (about 5 whole crackers)
- 1 tablespoon baking powder
- 1/2 teaspoon salt
- 3 tablespoons firmly packed brown sugar
- 1 stick (1/2 cup) cold unsalted butter, cut into bits
- 2/3 cup plus 1 tablespoon milk
- 2 teaspoons granulated sugar

- 1 cup well-chilled heavy cream
- 2 tablespoons confectioners' sugar
- 3 tablespoons sour cream

In a bowl combine one third of peaches with lemon juice, granulated sugar, and schnapps and mash lightly with a fork. Stir in remaining peaches and macerate, covered and chilled, stirring occasionally, 1 hour.

Make biscuits:

Preheat oven to 425° F. and butter a baking sheet.

In a bowl whisk together flour, crumbs, baking powder, and salt. Add brown sugar and butter and blend until mixture resembles coarse meal. Add milk and stir until mixture just forms a dough. Drop dough in 6 mounds 2 inches apart onto prepared sheet and sprinkle with granulated sugar. Bake biscuits in middle of oven 20 to 25 minutes, or until golden. Transfer biscuits carefully to a rack and cool. *Biscuits may be made 1 day ahead and kept, wrapped well, at room temperature.*

In a chilled bowl beat heavy cream with confectioners' sugar until it just holds soft peaks and beat in sour cream, beating until cream holds stiff peaks. Cut top one fourth off each biscuit with a serrated knife, transferring bottoms to

6 plates, and spoon peaches with liquid over bottoms. Top peaches with whipped cream and cover with biscuit tops. Serves 6.

Coconut Macaroon Torte

For torte

- 1 cup sweetened flaked coconut, lightly toasted and cooled
- 1/2 cup blanched almonds, toasted and cooled
- 3/4 cup sugar
- 1/3 cup all-purpose flour
- 1 stick (1/2 cup) unsalted butter, melted
- 2 tablespoons coconut-flavored rum
- 1/4 teaspoon almond extract
- 3/4 cup egg whites (from about 5 large eggs)
- 1/4 teaspoon salt

Accompaniments

fresh fruit such as strawberries, raspberries, sliced peaches, or orange sections

vanilla ice cream

Make torte:

Preheat oven to 375° F. and butter a 9-inch springform pan.

In a food processor or blender finely grind coconut and almonds with ½ cup sugar and transfer to a large bowl. Stir in flour, butter, rum, and almond extract. In a bowl beat whites with salt until they barely hold soft peaks. Add remaining ¼ cup sugar gradually and beat whites until they just hold stiff peaks. Stir one third of whites into coconut mixture to lighten and fold in remaining whites gently but thoroughly. Pour batter into prepared pan and bake in middle of oven 40 minutes, or until golden brown and a tester comes out clean. Cool torte in pan on a rack 10 minutes. Remove side of pan and invert torte onto rack. Remove bottom of pan from torte and cool torte completely. *Torte may be made 1 day ahead and kept, wrapped in plastic wrap, at room temperature.*

Top torte with fresh fruit and serve with vanilla ice cream.

Ohio Shaker Lemon Pie

      2 lemons
 1 3/4 cups sugar
        For pastry dough
 1 3/4 cups all-purpose flour
      9 tablespoons cold unsalted butter,
         cut into bits
      3 tablespoons cold vegetable shortening
         a scant 1/2 teaspoon salt
      3 tablespoons ice water

      4 large eggs
    1/4 teaspoon salt

In a saucepan of boiling water blanch lemons 30 seconds. Drain lemons and rinse under cold water. Trim ends of lemons and discard. Cut lemons crosswise into paper-thin slices and in a bowl cover with sugar. *Let lemon mixture stand, stirring once after 1 hour, for 8 hours or overnight.*

Make pastry dough:

In a bowl blend flour, butter, shortening, and salt until mixture resembles meal. Add 3 tablespoons ice water and toss until incorporated. Add additional ice water if necessary to form a dough and form into a disk. Lightly dust dough with flour and chill, wrapped in wax paper, 1 hour.

Preheat oven to 425° F.

Roll out half of dough ⅛ inch thick on a floured surface. Fit dough into a 9-inch (1-quart) pie plate and trim edge, leaving a ½-inch overhang. Remove lemon slices from sugar and arrange in shell. Add eggs and salt to sugar, whisking until combined well, and pour over lemons.

Roll out remaining dough into a 12-inch round on a lightly floured surface. Drape dough over filling and trim, leaving a 1-inch overhang. Fold overhang under bottom crust, pressing edge to seal, and crimp edge decoratively. Cut slits in crust with a sharp knife, forming steam vents, and bake in middle of oven 25 minutes.

Reduce temperature to 350° F.

Bake pie 20 minutes more, or until crust is golden. Cool pie on a rack.

Photo opposite

Gingered Pumpkin and Applesauce Pie

        For crust
      1 cup graham cracker crumbs
         (about 9 whole crackers)
      3 tablespoons unsalted butter, melted
      1 tablespoon granulated sugar
         For filling
    1/2 stick (1/4 cup) unsalted butter, softened
    1/2 cup firmly packed light brown sugar
      2 cups canned solid-pack pumpkin
 1 1/2 cups applesauce
      3 large eggs
    1/3 cup heavy cream
    1/3 cup light corn syrup
    1/4 cup brandy or orange juice
      1 tablespoon minced peeled fresh gingerroot
    1/4 teaspoon freshly grated nutmeg
         a pinch salt

Accompaniment: freshly whipped cream

Preheat oven to 425° F. and butter a 10-inch (1½-quart) pie plate.

Make crust:

In a bowl combine crust ingredients and press onto bottom and halfway up side of prepared pie plate.

Make filling:

In a large bowl with an electric mixer beat together butter and brown sugar until light and fluffy. Beat in canned pumpkin, applesauce, eggs, 1 at a time, and remaining ingredients until combined well.

Pour filling into crust and bake in middle of oven 10 minutes.

Reduce temperature to 325° F.

Bake pie 45 minutes more, or until a tester comes out clean. Cool pie on a rack.

Serve pie warm or chilled with freshly whipped cream.

Ohio Shaker Lemon Pie; Cranberry Raisin Tart (page 187)

Jumbleberry Pie

       2 recipes pastry dough (page 23)
          For filling
       3 cups blackberries, picked over and rinsed
       3 cups blueberries, picked over and rinsed
  2 1/2   cups raspberries or other summer berries
          such as red currants or boysenberries,
          picked over and rinsed
     1/3 cup cornstarch
   1 1/2 cups sugar
     1/4 cup fresh lemon juice
     1/8 teaspoon freshly grated nutmeg
     1/8 teaspoon cinnamon

       1 tablespoon unsalted butter, cut into bits
     1/4 cup half-and-half
          sugar for sprinkling pie

Accompaniment: **peach and brown sugar ice cream (recipe follows)**

Preheat oven to 425° F.

Roll out half of dough ⅛ inch thick on a lightly floured surface. Fit dough into a 9-inch deep-dish (1 quart) pie plate and trim edge, leaving a ½-inch overhang. Chill shell while making filling.

Make filling:

In a large bowl toss together filling ingredients until combined well.

Mound filling in shell and dot it with butter bits. Roll out remaining dough into a 13- to 14-inch round on a lightly floured surface. Drape dough over filling and trim, leaving a 1-inch overhang. Fold overhang under bottom crust, pressing edge to seal, and crimp edge decoratively. Brush crust with half-and-half. Make slits in top crust, forming steam vents, and sprinkle lightly with sugar. Bake pie on a large baking sheet in middle of oven 20 minutes.

Reduce temperature to 375° F.

Bake pie 35 to 40 minutes more, or until crust is golden and filling is bubbling.

Serve pie with ice cream.

Photo on page 8

Peach and Brown Sugar Ice Cream

       2 pounds very ripe peaches (about 4), pitted
          and chopped
       2 tablespoons granulated sugar
     1/2 cup water
     3/4 cup firmly packed light brown sugar
       3 large egg yolks plus 1 large whole egg
   1 1/2 cups half and half
     1/4 teaspoon cinnamon
     1/4 teaspoon freshly grated nutmeg
       2 tablespoons peach schnapps or
          peach-flavored liqueur

In a saucepan combine peaches, granulated sugar, and ¼ cup water and simmer, stirring occasionally, 15 to 20 minutes, or until peaches are soft. Purée mixture in a food processor or blender. Force purée through a fine sieve into a bowl and cool. In another saucepan cook brown sugar and remaining ¼ cup water over moderately low heat, stirring, until sugar is dissolved.

In a large bowl with an electric mixer beat yolks and whole egg until frothy. Beat in brown sugar syrup and beat until thick and pale. In a small saucepan scald half-and-half and stir into brown sugar mixture. Pour mixture into pan and cook over moderately low heat, stirring with a wooden spoon, until it reaches 175° F. on a candy thermometer.

Strain custard through fine sieve into another large bowl and cool. Stir in peach purée and remaining ingredients and freeze in an ice-cream maker. Makes about 1 quart.

Photo on page 8

Blueberry Buttermilk Tart

For shell

1 1/3 cups all-purpose flour
1/4 cup granulated sugar
1/4 teaspoon salt
1 stick (1/2 cup) cold unsalted butter,
   cut into bits
1 large egg yolk beaten with
   2 tablespoons ice water
   raw rice for weighting shell
   For buttermilk filling
1 cup buttermilk
3 large egg yolks
1/2 cup granulated sugar
1 tablespoon freshly grated lemon zest
1 tablespoon fresh lemon juice
1/2 stick (1/4 cup) unsalted butter,
   melted and cooled
1 teaspoon vanilla
1/2 teaspoon salt
2 tablespoons all-purpose flour

2 cups picked-over blueberries

Garnish: confectioners' sugar
Accompaniment: blueberry ice cream
(recipe follows)

Make shell:

In a bowl stir together flour, sugar, and salt. Add butter and blend until mixture resembles coarse meal. Add yolk mixture, tossing until liquid is incorporated, and form dough into a disk. Dust dough with flour and chill, wrapped in plastic wrap, 1 hour. Roll out dough ⅛ inch thick on a floured surface and fit into a 10-inch tart pan with a removable fluted rim. *Chill shell at least 30 minutes or, covered, overnight.*

Preheat oven to 350° F.

Line shell with foil and fill with rice. Bake shell in middle of oven 25 minutes. Remove foil and rice carefully and bake shell 5 minutes more, or until pale golden. Cool shell in pan on a rack.

Make buttermilk filling:

In a blender or food processor blend together filling ingredients until smooth.

Spread blueberries evenly in bottom of shell. Pour buttermilk filling over blueberries and bake in middle of oven 30 to 35 minutes, or until just set. Remove rim of pan and cool tart completely in pan on rack.

Sift confectioners' sugar over tart and serve at room temperature or chilled with blueberry ice cream.

Photo on page 174

Blueberry Ice Cream

4 cups picked-over blueberries
1 cup sugar
   zest of 1 navel orange removed in strips
   with a vegetable peeler
1/4 cup water
2 tablespoons Grand Marnier or other
   orange-flavored liqueur
3 tablespoons fresh lemon juice
1/2 teaspoon vanilla
1/8 teaspoon salt
2 cups heavy cream
1 cup half-and-half

In a large saucepan bring blueberries, sugar, zest, and water to a boil and boil, covered, stirring occasionally, 5 minutes. Simmer mixture, uncovered, 5 minutes. Discard zest and in a blender or food processor purée mixture in batches. Transfer purée to a bowl and whisk in remaining ingredients. Force mixture through a very fine sieve into another bowl and chill, covered, 1 hour, or until cold. Freeze mixture in an ice-cream maker. Makes about 1½ quarts.

Photo on page 174

Banana Cream Tart

For crust

3/4 stick (6 tablespoons) unsalted butter, melted and cooled

2 cups graham cracker crumbs (about 18 whole crackers)

For filling

1/3 cup sugar

3 tablespoons cornstarch

1/8 teaspoon salt

3 large eggs, beaten lightly

2 cups milk

1/2 vanilla bean, split lengthwise

6 bananas

3/4 cup apricot jam

Make crust:

In a bowl stir together butter and graham cracker crumbs and press onto bottom and up side of a 10-inch tart pan with a removable rim. Chill crust while making filling.

Make filling:

In a bowl whisk together sugar, corn-starch, and salt and whisk in eggs. In a heavy saucepan heat milk over moderately high heat until it just comes to a boil and add to egg mixture in a slow stream, whisking until smooth. Transfer custard to pan and scrape seeds from vanilla bean into it, reserving pod for another use. Bring custard to a boil over moderate heat, whisking constantly. Simmer custard, whisking, 2 minutes and transfer to a bowl. *Chill custard, its surface covered with plastic wrap, at least 4 hours, or until cold, and up to 1 day.*

Chop 2 bananas and scatter into crust. Cover bananas with custard, spreading evenly. Slice remaining 6 bananas diagonally and arrange, overlapping slightly, on top of custard, covering it entirely. In a small saucepan melt apricot jam over moderate heat and strain through a fine sieve into a bowl. Brush warm jam over bananas, coating them completely, and chill tart 1 hour. *Tart may be made 1 day ahead and chilled, covered loosely.*

Chocolate Raspberry Tart

For crust

1 1/4 cups all-purpose flour

3/4 cup walnut pieces

1 stick (1/2 cup) cold unsalted butter, cut into bits

2 tablespoons sugar

3/4 teaspoon salt

1/2 teaspoon cinnamon

For chocolate filling

1/3 cup heavy cream

9 ounces fine-quality bittersweet chocolate (not unsweetened), chopped fine

3 tablespoons unsalted butter, cut into bits and softened

1/3 cup seedless red raspberry jam

For topping

1/4 cup seedless red raspberry jam

3 cups fresh raspberries (three 1/2 pints)

Make crust:

Preheat oven to 375° F.

In a food processor blend crust ingredients until mixture just forms a ball. Pat mixture evenly into an 11-inch tart pan with a removable fluted rim and freeze 15 minutes, or until firm. Bake crust in oven 20 minutes, or until lightly browned, and cool in pan on a rack.

Make chocolate filling:

In a saucepan bring cream just to a boil over moderate heat and remove pan from heat. Add chocolate, stirring until completely melted and mixture is smooth. Cool mixture slightly and add butter, bit by bit, stirring until smooth. Stir in jam and a pinch salt.

Spread filling in crust and chill, covered, 4 hours, or until firm. Remove rim of pan and transfer tart to a serving plate.

Make topping:

In a bowl whisk jam until smooth. Add raspberries and toss to coat well.

Spoon raspberry topping evenly over chocolate filling. *Tart may be made 2 days ahead and chilled, covered.*

Serve tart cut into thin wedges.

Cranberry Raisin Tart

For filling
3/4 cup firmly packed light brown sugar
1 tablespoon cornstarch
1 teaspoon freshly grated orange zest
1/4 cup fresh orange juice
2 cups cranberries, picked over
1 cup golden raisins, soaked in hot water
5 minutes and drained
1/4 teaspoon salt
For dough
1 1/4 cups all-purpose flour
3 tablespoons granulated sugar
1/4 teaspoon baking powder
1/8 teaspoon salt
3/4 stick (6 tablespoons) cold unsalted butter,
cut into bits
1 large egg beaten with 1 tablespoon water

egg wash made by beating 1 egg with
1 tablespoon water

Make filling:
In a saucepan combine filling ingredients. Bring mixture to a boil, stirring, and simmer, stirring, 5 minutes, or until berries just burst. Transfer filling to a bowl and cool. *Chill filling, covered, at least 2 hours, or until cold, and up to 2 days.*

Make dough:
In a bowl stir together flour, granulated sugar, baking powder, and salt. Add butter and blend until mixture resembles meal. Add egg mixture, stirring with a fork until mixture just forms a dough. Form dough into a disk and dust with flour. Chill dough, wrapped in wax paper, 1 hour.

Preheat oven to 425° F.

Roll out dough into a 12-inch round on a lightly floured surface and transfer to a baking sheet. Spoon filling onto center of dough, spreading it into an 8-inch circle, and fold edges of dough over it, leaving center of filling uncovered. Brush dough with egg wash and bake in middle of oven, covering exposed filling loosely with foil after 10 minutes, 15 to 20 minutes, or until pastry is golden. Cool tart on baking sheet on a rack.

Photo on page 183

Apricot Puff Pastry Tarts

2 sheets frozen puff pastry
(about 1 pound), thawed
2 pounds firm-ripe apricots, halved,
pitted, and sliced thin
6 tablespoons sugar
1 teaspoon cinnamon
1/2 cup apricot jam, melted and cooled

Accompaniment: vanilla ice cream
or whipped cream

Preheat oven to 400° F.

Roll out each puff pastry sheet on a lightly floured surface into a 10-inch square, about 1/8 inch thick. Transfer pastry squares to 2 shallow baking pans and freeze 5 minutes. Arrange apricot slices, overlapping slightly, on squares, leaving a 1/2-inch border all around. In a small bowl stir together sugar and cinnamon and sprinkle evenly over each tart.

Bake tarts in middle and lower third of oven, switching position of pans halfway through baking, 25 to 30 minutes, or until pastry is golden brown. Brush tarts with jam.

Serve tarts warm or at room temperature with ice cream or whipped cream. Makes 2 tarts, serving 6.

Mango Lemon Mousse

1	envelope (1 tablespoon) unflavored gelatin
1/4	cup cold water
6	large egg yolks
3/4	cup sugar
1/3	cup fresh lemon juice
2	cups fresh mango purée (from about 3 to 4 ripe mangoes)
1	cup well-chilled heavy cream

In a bowl sprinkle gelatin over water and soften.

In a small heavy saucepan whisk together yolks and sugar and whisk in lemon juice. Cook mixture over moderately low heat, whisking constantly, until it registers 170° F. on a candy thermometer, about 15 minutes (do not let it boil). Strain custard through a fine sieve into a bowl and stir in gelatin mixture, stirring until dissolved. Stir in mango purée. Cool mango mixture, its surface covered with plastic wrap, and chill until cold but not set, about 15 minutes.

In another bowl beat cream until it holds stiff peaks. Whisk one fourth of cream into mango mixture to lighten and fold in remaining cream gently but thoroughly. Divide mousse among 6 serving glasses. *Chill mousse, its surface covered with plastic wrap, at least 8 hours and up to 2 days.* Serves 6.

◔+ Macerated Cherries

2	pounds fresh sweet cherries, pitted
1/4	cup orange-flavored liqueur, kirsch, or Cognac
2	tablespoons fresh lemon juice, or to taste
2 1/2	tablespoons brown sugar, or to taste

Accompaniment: toasted blanched almonds, ice cream, or lightly whipped cream

In a large ceramic or glass bowl toss cherries with remaining ingredients. *Macerate cherries, covered, at least 2 hours or overnight.*

Serve cherries with almonds, ice cream, or whipped cream. Serves 6.

◔+ Mint Chocolate Meringue Mousses

4	ounces fine-quality bittersweet chocolate (not unsweetened), chopped
2	tablespoons green *crème de menthe*
2	large egg yolks
2/3	cup sugar
1/3	cup water
4	large egg whites

Garnish: whipped cream, chocolate curls, and green *crème de menthe*

In a heatproof bowl set over barely simmering water melt chocolate with *crème de menthe*, whisking, and remove from heat. Whisk in yolks, 1 at a time, until combined well and cool. In a small heavy saucepan bring sugar and water to a boil, stirring until sugar is dissolved. Boil syrup until it registers 248° F. on a candy thermometer and remove pan from heat.

While syrup is boiling, in a bowl with an electric mixer beat whites with a pinch salt until they hold soft peaks. With mixer on medium speed add hot syrup in a stream and beat until cool. Whisk about 1 cup meringue into chocolate mixture to lighten and fold into remaining meringue gently but thoroughly. Divide mousse among 6 serving glasses. *Chill mousse, covered, at least 2 hours or overnight.*

Just before serving, garnish mousses with whipped cream, chocolate curls, and a drizzle of *crème de menthe.* Serves 6.

Almond Meringue Kisses

For meringues
1 cup almonds
1 cup sugar
1 tablespoon cornstarch
4 large egg whites
1/8 teaspoon salt
1/4 teaspoon almond or vanilla extract
For ganache
1/3 cup heavy cream
3/4 cup semisweet chocolate chips

Make meringues:

Preheat oven to 325° F. and line a baking sheet with parchment paper.

In a food processor grind almonds fine with ¼ cup sugar and cornstarch. In a large bowl beat whites with salt and extract until they hold soft peaks. Add remaining ¾ cup sugar gradually, beating until very stiff and glossy. Fold in almond mixture and with a 2½- by 1¾-inch oval ice cream scoop drop meringue in 24 mounds onto prepared sheet. Bake meringues in middle of oven 25 to 30 minutes, or until just firm to the touch and lightly colored. Cool meringues on parchment and peel off carefully.

Make ganache:

In a small saucepan bring cream just to a boil over moderate heat. Remove pan from heat and add chips. Stir *ganache* until smooth and cool, stirring occasionally, until of spreading consistency.

Spread *ganache* on bottoms of half of meringues and attach remaining meringues to *ganache* to form sandwiches. Chill sandwiches 15 minutes. *Cookie sandwiches may be made 5 days ahead and chilled in an airtight container.* Makes 12 cookie sandwiches.

Caramel Crème Caramel

1 cup sugar
2 3/4 cups half-and-half
3 large whole eggs plus 4 large egg yolks
2 teaspoons vanilla
1/2 teaspoon salt

Preheat oven to 325° F.

In a saucepan cook ¼ cup sugar over moderate heat, without stirring, until it begins to melt. Continue to cook sugar, stirring occasionally, until a deep golden caramel and pour immediately into a 4- to 5-cup flat-bottomed ring mold. Swirl mold to coat side slightly and set mold in a large baking pan. Let caramel harden.

To same saucepan add remaining ¾ cup sugar and cook over moderate heat, without stirring, until it begins to melt. Continue to cook sugar, stirring occasionally, until a deep golden caramel. In a heavy saucepan scald half-and-half over moderate heat and add to caramel in saucepan. Cook half-and-half mixture, stirring, until caramel is dissolved and remove pan from heat. In a large bowl whisk together remaining ingredients. Add half-and-half mixture in a stream, whisking, and strain through a fine sieve into mold.

Cover mold tightly with foil and put baking pan with mold in middle of oven. Add enough hot water to pan to reach halfway up side of mold and bake *crème caramel* 45 minutes, or until just set.

Remove mold from pan. Remove foil and cool *crème caramel* in mold on a rack. *Chill* crème caramel, *covered, at least 3 hours, or until cold and completely set, and up to 1 day.*

Dip mold in hot water 30 seconds and run a thin knife around side and center of ring mold. Invert a platter over mold and invert *crème caramel* onto it. Serves 6.

Coconut Parfaits

2 cups milk
2/3 cup heavy cream
3 large eggs, lightly beaten
1 1/2 cups canned cream of coconut
4 1/2 tablespoons coconut-flavored rum if desired

Garnish: 1 1/2 cups sweetened flaked coconut, lightly toasted

In a heavy saucepan bring milk and cream just to a boil and in a bowl add in a slow stream to eggs, whisking. Transfer egg mixture to pan and cook over moderately low heat, stirring constantly with a wooden spoon, until thickened (175° F. on a candy thermometer), but do not let it boil. Remove pan from heat and strain custard through a fine sieve into a metal bowl set in a larger bowl of ice and cold water. Stir in cream of coconut and rum. Cool custard, stirring occasionally, until cold and freeze in an ice-cream maker. *Freeze ice cream in a freezer container at least until firm and up to 1 week.*

Scoop ice cream with a small scoop into 6 parfait glasses, sprinkling each scoop with toasted coconut. Serves 6.

Photo opposite

☺+ Rum Raisin Ice Cream

1/3 cup dark rum
1/2 teaspoon cinnamon
1 1/3 cups packed golden raisins
1/4 teaspoon rum extract
2 pints premium-quality vanilla ice cream or frozen yogurt, softened

In a saucepan simmer rum with cinnamon and raisins, stirring, until raisins are plumped, about 2 minutes, and cool slightly. In a large bowl whisk raisins and rum extract into ice cream or frozen yogurt until combined well. *Freeze ice cream or frozen yogurt in a freezer container at least 2 hours and up to 1 week.* Serves 6.

Rosé Sorbet; Coconut Parfait

☺+ Raspberry Rhubarb Yogurt Parfaits

3 pints vanilla yogurt
1 pound rhubarb, trimmed and cut into 3/4-inch pieces (about 3 1/2 cups)
3/4 cup sugar
1/4 cup fresh orange juice
3/4 pint raspberries

Garnish: raspberries

Set a large sieve, lined with rinsed and squeezed cheesecloth, over a bowl and add yogurt. *Drain yogurt, covered and chilled, 8 hours or overnight.*

In a heavy saucepan simmer rhubarb, sugar, and orange juice, stirring occasionally, 5 to 10 minutes, or until rhubarb is tender and transfer to a bowl. Stir in raspberries and cool. *Chill fruit mixture, covered, at least 2 hours or overnight.*

Spoon alternating layers of yogurt and fruit mixture into 6 parfait or other stemmed glasses and garnish with raspberries. Serves 6.

☺+ Rosé Sorbet

3 3/4 cups medium-dry rosé wine
1 1/2 cups water
1 1/2 cups sugar
3 tablespoons fresh lemon juice, or to taste

Garnish: 6 mint sprigs

In a saucepan bring wine to a boil and simmer 5 minutes. Pour rosé wine into a metal bowl set in a larger bowl of ice and cold water. In pan bring 1½ cups water to a boil with sugar, stirring until sugar is dissolved, and stir into wine. Let mixture stand, stirring occasionally, until cold and stir in lemon juice. Freeze mixture in an ice-cream maker. *Freeze rosé sorbet in a freezer container at least until firm and up to 1 week.*

Scoop sorbet with a small scoop into 6 parfait glasses and garnish with mint. Serves 6.

Photo opposite

more
snacks &
beverages

Yellow Bell Pepper Salsa with Cumin Tortilla Chips;
Chili Almonds and Coconut Chips (page 199)

☺+ Roasted Garlic

6   heads of garlic, unpeeled
1   bay leaf
2   tablespoons olive oil
1/4   cup chicken broth

Accompaniments
slices of crusty bread or *baguette*
assorted cheeses such as goat cheese,
Brie, or Gorgonzola
fruit such as grapes, sliced apples, or pears

Preheat oven to 400° F. and line a baking dish just large enough to hold garlic heads in one layer with a sheet of foil.

Cut off top third of each garlic head to expose cloves and arrange, cut sides up, in prepared dish with bay leaf. Drizzle garlic with oil and broth and season with salt and pepper. Cover dish tightly with foil and bake garlic in middle of oven 1 hour, or until garlic skin is browned and cloves are soft.

To serve, squeeze garlic from cloves and spread on bread. Top garlic with cheese and/or fruit. Serves 6.

Sesame Batter-Fried Chicken Strips

For batter
1   large egg, beaten lightly
1/2   cup milk
1   teaspoon salt
1   garlic clove, minced
1/2   to 3/4 cup all-purpose flour

1   teaspoon baking powder
vegetable shortening for deep frying
1/4   cup sesame seeds
3   whole boneless skinless chicken breasts, cut into 1/2-inch strips

Accompaniments
Chinese duck sauce*
Chinese mustard*

*available at Asian markets and some specialty foods shops and supermarkets

Make batter:
In a bowl whisk together egg, milk, salt, and minced garlic and whisk in enough flour, ¼ cup at a time, to form a batter of coating consistency. *Let batter stand, covered, at room temperature 1 hour or chilled overnight.*

Whisk baking powder into batter and let stand 15 minutes. In a deep fryer or large deep kettle heat 3 inches shortening over moderately high heat until it registers 375° F. on a deep-fat thermometer. Spread sesame seeds on a plate and stir batter. Pat chicken strips dry and add to batter. Working in batches of 6 strips, dip one side of each strip lightly into sesame seeds and fry in oil 1 minute, or until golden and cooked through, making sure oil returns to 375° F. before adding each new batch. Transfer chicken strips as fried with a skimmer or slotted spoon to paper towels to drain.

Serve chicken strips with Chinese duck sauce and mustard. Makes about 36 snacks or hors d'oeuvres.

Cheddar Potato Skins with Chutney

1   8 1/2-ounce jar mango chutney
1   to 2 *jalapeño* chilies, seeded and minced,
    or to taste (wear rubber gloves)
6   baked scrubbed potatoes, quartered
    (into 24 wedges) and potato scooped
    out, leaving 1/2 inch-thick potato-lined skins
2 1/4   cups coarsely grated sharp Cheddar cheese
    (about 8 ounces)

Preheat oven to 450° F. and butter a shallow baking pan.

In a food processor purée chutney until smooth and transfer to a bowl. Stir in *jalapeños*.

Arrange skins in one layer in prepared pan and season with salt and pepper. Sprinkle Cheddar evenly on top of skins. *Skins may be prepared up to this point 3 hours ahead and chilled, covered.* Bake skins in middle of oven 5 to 8 minutes, or until crisp and cheese is bubbling.

Serve skins topped with chutney purée. Makes 24 snacks or hors d'oeuvres.

☺+ Marinated Shrimp and Onions

1 1/4   pounds medium shrimp (about 40)
1   tablespoon mustard seeds
1   tablespoon coriander seeds
1/3   cup rice vinegar*
1   teaspoon salt
2   garlic cloves, minced
3/4   teaspoon freshly grated lemon zest
3/4   teaspoon dried hot red pepper flakes
2   tablespoons drained bottled capers
1   yellow bell pepper, cut into 1-inch strips
1/4   cup olive oil
1/2   cup drained bottled cocktail onions
    (about 4 ounces), halved lengthwise
    and rinsed well

Accompaniment: crackers or toast points

*available at Asian markets and some supermarkets

Bring a kettle of salted water to a boil for shrimp.

With a mortar and pestle lightly bruise seeds, but do not pulverize them.

In a bowl whisk together vinegar, bruised seeds, salt, garlic, zest, red pepper flakes, capers, and bell pepper. Add oil in a stream, whisking, and whisk until combined well. Stir in onions.

In boiling water cook shrimp 1 minute, or until pink and firm, and drain. Cool shrimp. Shell shrimp and if desired devein. Add shrimp to marinade and toss to combine well. Transfer mixture to a resealable plastic bag. *Marinate shrimp, chilled, at least 8 hours or overnight.*

Serve shrimp and onions with crackers or toast points. Serves 6 to 8.

Cheddar Twists

   quick puff paste (recipe follows)
   an egg wash made by beating 1 large
   egg with 2 teaspoons water
3 cups coarsely grated sharp Cheddar cheese
   coarse salt for sprinkling dough

Preheat oven to 425° F. and grease a baking sheet.

Halve dough and reserve 1 half, wrapped and chilled. On a lightly floured surface roll out remaining dough into an 18- by 12-inch rectangle. Brush dough with some egg wash and sprinkle lightly with pepper. Sprinkle half of Cheddar over a crosswise half of dough and fold plain half of dough over Cheddar, pressing firmly to force out air. Roll out dough slightly to make layers adhere. Brush dough with some remaining egg wash and sprinkle lightly with coarse salt. With a pastry wheel or knife cut dough lengthwise into ½-inch-thick strips. Twist strips and arrange on prepared baking sheet, pressing ends onto sheet. Bake twists in middle of oven 12 to 15 minutes, or until pale golden. Make more Cheddar twists in same manner with remaining ingredients. *Twists may be made 3 days ahead and kept in an airtight container.* Makes about 36 twists.

Photo opposite

Quick Puff Paste

  2 cups all-purpose flour sifted
     with 1/2 teaspoon salt
1 3/4 sticks (3/4 cup plus 2 tablespoons)
     cold unsalted butter, cut into bits
  1/3 to 1/2 cup ice water

In a large bowl blend flour mixture and butter until mixture resembles meal and add enough ice water to just form a dough. Form dough into a ball and dust with flour. Chill dough, wrapped in wax paper, 1 hour.

On a floured surface roll out dough into a 12- by 6-inch rectangle, dusting with flour if it sticks to rolling pin. Fold top third of rectangle over center and bottom third over top, forming a rectangle about 6 by 4 inches. Press down top edge with rolling pin so it adheres and turn dough seam side down. Brush any excess flour from dough. With an open side facing you roll dough out again into a 12- by 6-inch rectangle and fold into thirds as before. This completes 2 "turns." Make 2 more turns, always starting with seam side down and open end facing you. *Chill dough, wrapped in wax paper, at least 30 minutes or up to 1 week.*

Pimm's Cups (page 204); Cheddar Twists

◔ Cheese Quesadillas

8 7- to 8-inch or four 10-inch flour tortillas
2 cups coarsely grated Monterey Jack
   or pepper Jack cheese (about 1/2 pound)
2 to 3 tablespoons vegetable oil for
   brushing tortillas

Accompaniments
guacamole (recipe follows)
tomato *salsa* (recipe follows
or store-bought)

Preheat broiler.

Arrange half of tortillas in one layer on a large baking sheet. Divide cheese evenly among them and top with remaining tortillas. Brush tops lightly with oil and broil under broiler about 2 inches from heat 1 minute, or until tops are golden and crisp. Turn *quesadillas* carefully with a spatula and brush tops with more oil. Broil *quesadillas* 1 minute more, or until tops are golden and crisp.

Serve *quesadillas*, cut into wedges, with *guacamole* and *salsa*. Serves 6 to 8 as a snack or hors d'oeuvre.

◔ Guacamole

2 ripe avocados (preferably California)
1 small onion, minced
1 garlic clove, minced and mashed to
   a paste with 1/2 teaspoon salt
4 teaspoons fresh lime juice, or to taste
1/2 teaspoon ground cumin
1 fresh or pickled *jalapeño* chili if desired,
   seeded and minced (wear rubber gloves)
3 tablespoons chopped fresh
   coriander if desired

Halve and pit avocados and scoop flesh into a bowl. Mash avocados coarse with a fork and stir in remaining ingredients. Guacamole *may be made 2 hours ahead and chilled, its surface covered with plastic wrap.* Makes about 2 cups.

◔ Tomato Salsa

1 pound tomatoes, peeled if desired,
   seeded and chopped
1 small onion, minced
1 fresh or pickled *jalapeño* chili, or to taste,
   seeded and minced (wear rubber gloves)
1 tablespoon fresh lime juice
2 tablespoons chopped fresh
   coriander if desired

In a bowl toss together all ingredients with salt to taste. Salsa *may be made 4 hours ahead and chilled, covered.* Let *salsa* stand at room temperature 30 minutes before serving. Makes about 2 cups.

Chili Almonds and Coconut Chips

1	coconut without any cracks and containing liquid
1 1/2	tablespoons fresh lemon juice
2	teaspoons chili powder
	cayenne to taste
1	cup sliced almonds

Preheat oven to 400° F.

With an ice pick or a skewer test 3 eyes of coconut to find weakest one and pierce it to make a hole. Drain liquid into a bowl and reserve for another use. Bake coconut in middle of oven 15 minutes and break with a hammer. With point of a strong small knife lever flesh carefully out of shell. With a vegetable peeler shave enough 1-inch-long slices of coconut to measure 1 cup, reserving remaining coconut for another use.

Reduce temperature to 350° F.

In a bowl toss coconut slices with half of lemon juice, half of chili powder, some cayenne, and salt to taste until coated well and transfer to a shallow baking pan. Bake slices in middle of oven, stirring occasionally, 12 to 15 minutes, or until golden, and transfer to a bowl. In another bowl toss almonds with remaining lemon juice, remaining chili powder, and cayenne and salt to taste until coated well and transfer to same baking pan. Bake almonds in oven, stirring occasionally, 8 to 10 minutes, or until golden. Toss coconut with almonds. *Almonds and coconut chips may be made 6 hours ahead and kept in an airtight container.* Makes about 2 cups.

Photo on page 192

◐+ Yellow Bell Pepper Salsa with Cumin Tortilla Chips

1 1/2	teaspoons ground cumin
1	teaspoon salt
	vegetable oil for frying tortillas
9	6-inch corn tortillas, each cut into 8 wedges

For salsa

2	small yellow bell peppers, chopped fine
1	avocado (preferably California), chopped fine
1	onion, chopped fine
2	tomatoes (about 1 pound), seeded and chopped fine
1	small purple or red bell pepper, chopped fine
1	2-inch fresh *jalapeño* chili including seeds, minced (wear rubber gloves)
1/2	cup lightly packed fresh coriander, chopped fine
3	tablespoons fresh lime juice
2	tablespoons fresh lemon juice

In a small bowl combine well cumin and salt. In a large deep heavy skillet heat ¾ inch of oil over moderately high heat until it registers 375° F. on a deep-fat thermometer and fry tortilla wedges in batches 30 seconds to 1 minute, or until crisp and most of bubbling subsides. Transfer chips as fried with a slotted spoon to paper towels to drain and sprinkle while warm with cumin mixture. *Tortilla chips may be made 1 day ahead and kept in an airtight container.*

Make salsa:

In a bowl combine well *salsa* ingredients. Chill *salsa*, its surface covered with plastic wrap, at least 1 hour and up to 6 hours.

Serve *salsa* with chips. Makes about 4½ cups.

Photo on page 192

☻ Prosciutto and Arugula Sandwich Bites with Olive Butter

- 1/2 stick (1/4 cup) unsalted butter, softened
- 2 tablespoons minced fresh parsley leaves
- 1/2 cup finely chopped pimiento-stuffed green olives
- fresh lemon juice to taste
- Tabasco to taste
- 2 12-inch *baguettes* or loaves of Italian bread, split lengthwise
- 1/2 pound thinly sliced prosciutto
- 1 bunch *arugula*, washed well and spun dry

In a small bowl with a fork blend together butter, parsley, olives, lemon juice, Tabasco, and salt and pepper to taste. Spread cut sides of bread with butter mixture and arrange prosciutto and *arugula* evenly on bottom halves of bread. Top fillings with top halves of bread, pressing down firmly, and cut crosswise into 1½-inch-thick slices. Makes 16 sandwich bites.

☻ Parmesan Pita Crisps

- 6 6-inch pita loaves
- about 1/4 cup olive oil
- 1 1/2 cups finely shredded Parmesan cheese (about 6 ounces)

Preheat oven to 375° F.

Split each pita loaf horizontally into 2 rounds and brush rough sides with oil. Cut each round into 16 wedges and arrange with edges touching, oiled sides up, on 2 baking sheets. Sprinkle with Parmesan and salt and pepper to taste and bake on middle and lower racks of oven, switching position of sheets in oven halfway through baking, 12 to 15 minutes, or until golden. *Crisps may be made 3 days ahead and kept in an airtight container.* Serves 12 as a snack or hors d'oeuvre.

White Bean Dip

3	cups drained cooked Great Northern or white kidney beans (procedure follows)
1/2	cup sour cream
1	garlic clove, minced
1	scallion, chopped
2	tablespoons minced fresh parsley leaves
2	tablespoons soy sauce
1/2	cup fresh lemon juice
1	tablespoon Dijon mustard
1/3	cup vegetable oil

Garnish: 1 tablespoon minced fresh parsley leaves

Accompaniment: pita toasts or corn tortilla chips

In a food processor or blender purée all ingredients except oil until smooth. With motor running add oil in a stream and blend until combined well. Transfer dip to a serving bowl and chill, covered, 2 hours.

Garnish dip with parsley and serve with toasts or chips. Makes about 3½ cups.

To Cook Dried White Beans

1/2	pound dried Great Northern or white kidney beans
2	cups chicken broth
6	cups water

In a kettle combine all ingredients. Bring liquid to a boil over moderate heat and boil 1 hour, or until beans are very tender. Drain beans. Makes about 3 cups.

Lentil Hummus

1	cup lentils, picked over and rinsed
3 1/2	cups water
1	onion stuck with a clove
3	garlic cloves
	a cheesecloth bag containing 4 parsley sprigs, 1 bay leaf, and 1/4 teaspoon dried thyme
1 1/2	teaspoons salt
1/3	cup fresh lemon juice plus additional to taste
1/3	cup *tahini** (sesame paste)
1/4	cup olive oil, or to taste, plus additional to cover *hummus*
	cayenne to taste

Garnish: minced fresh parsley leaves

Accompaniment: pita loaves, cut into wedges and lightly toasted

*available at specialty foods shops and natural foods stores

In a heavy saucepan cover lentils with water and add cloved onion, 1 garlic clove, and cheesecloth bag. Bring water to a boil and simmer, partially covered, 45 minutes, or until lentils are tender. Add salt and simmer 5 minutes. Discard onion and cheesecloth bag and drain lentils.

Into a food processor or blender with motor running drop remaining 2 garlic cloves and mince fine. With motor running add ⅓ cup lemon juice and purée mixture. Add lentils in batches and blend alternately with well-stirred *tahini.* With motor running add ¼ cup oil, or to taste, in a stream and blend until smooth. Season *hummus* with additional lemon juice, cayenne, and salt and pepper to taste. Transfer *hummus* to a ceramic or glass serving bowl and cover with a thin layer of additional oil.

Garnish *hummus* with parsley and serve with pita wedges. Makes about 3½ cups.

Blue Lagoon (Blue Curaçao and Vodka Cocktail)

1 1/2   ounces (1 jigger) vodka
1   ounce (1 pony) blue Curaçao
1/3   cup lemonade (recipe follows)

In a long-stemmed glass filled with ice cubes stir together all ingredients. Makes 1 drink.
Photo opposite

Lemonade

1   cup fresh lemon juice
2   cups cold water
1/3   cup sugar, or to taste
6   thin lemon slices

In a pitcher stir together lemon juice, water, and sugar until sugar is dissolved. Add lemon slices and chill, covered. Makes about 3¼ cups.

Mango Wine Cooler

1/2   cup chilled dry white wine
1   ounce (1 pony) Mohala (mango liqueur)
1/4   pitted and peeled mango, cut into strips, reserving 1 strip for garnish

In a tall glass filled with ice cubes stir together wine, Mohala, and mango. Garnish drink with reserved mango strip. Makes 1 drink.
Photo opposite

Melon Ball (Midori and Vodka Cocktail)

1 1/2   ounces (1 jigger) Midori (melon-flavored liqueur)
1 1/2   ounces (1 jigger) vodka
1/3   cup strained fresh orange juice

Garnish: a bamboo skewer threaded with 3 melon balls

In a long-stemmed glass filled with ice cubes stir together all ingredients. Garnish drink with melon skewer. Makes 1 drink.
Photo opposite

Planter's Punch

2/3   cup dark rum
1/4   cup fresh lime juice
1/4   cup triple sec
1   tablespoon grenadine
1/2   teaspoon Angostura bitters
1/2   cup fresh orange juice

Garnish: 4 lime slices and 4 bamboo skewers, each threaded with a lime wedge, an orange wedge, and a maraschino cherry

In a cocktail shaker half-filled with ice cubes combine all ingredients and shake 30 seconds. Strain drink into 4 tall glasses filled with ice cubes and garnish with lime slices and fruit skewers. Makes 4 drinks.
Photo opposite

Left to right: Mango Wine Cooler; Blue Lagoon; Planter's Punch; and Melon Ball

Pimm's Cup

1 1/2 ounces (1 jigger) Pimm's No. 1 Cup
1 lengthwise strip of cucumber peel
1 apple wedge
   chilled club soda or seltzer
   chilled ginger ale

Garnish: 1 lemon slice

In a glass filled with ice cubes combine Pimm's, cucumber peel, and apple. Top off mixture with equal parts club soda or seltzer and ginger ale and stir well. Garnish drink with lemon slice. Makes 1 drink.
Photo on page 197

Sea Breeze

1 1/2 ounces (1 jigger) vodka
1/4 cup chilled grapefruit juice
1/4 cup chilled cranberry juice

Garnish: 1 small grapefruit wedge

In a long-stemmed glass filled with ice cubes stir together all ingredients. Garnish drink with grapefruit wedge. Makes 1 drink.

Spiced Cranberry Rum Tea

1 1/2 cups boiling water
4 cranberry herb tea bags such as Celestial Seasonings brand
1/3 cup sugar
1/2 cup cranberry juice
4 to 6 whole star anise*
2 3-inch strips of orange zest removed with a vegetable peeler
2 3-inch strips of lemon zest removed with a vegetable peeler
1 cup strained fresh orange juice
1 cup amber rum, or to taste

Garnish: lemon slices

*available at specialty foods shops and Asian markets

In a saucepan bring water to a boil. Submerge tea bags in water and remove pan from heat. Let tea bags steep 5 minutes and discard. To tea add sugar, cranberry juice, star anise, and zests and simmer, covered, stirring occasionally, 10 minutes. Stir in orange juice and rum and heat over moderate heat until hot. Discard zests and divide tea among heated mugs. Garnish each drink with a star anise and a lemon slice. Makes about 4½ cups, serving 4 to 6.

Mojito (Rum, Lemon, and Mint Cocktail)

2 fresh mint sprigs
2 teaspoons sugar
2 tablespoons fresh lemon juice
1 1/2 ounces (1 jigger) light rum
chilled club soda or seltzer

Garnish: fresh mint sprig and lemon slices

In a tall glass with back of a spoon crush mint sprigs with sugar and lemon juice until sugar is dissolved and add rum. Add ice cubes and top off drink with club soda or seltzer. Stir drink well and garnish with fresh mint sprig and lemon slices. Makes 1 drink.

Orange-, Grapefruit-, and Lemon-ade

2 cups water
3/4 cup plus 3 tablespoons sugar, or to taste
1 1/4 cups fresh orange juice
1 1/4 cups fresh grapefruit juice
1 1/4 cups fresh lemon juice

Garnish: 6 fresh mint sprigs

In a small saucepan stir together water and sugar and bring to a boil, stirring until sugar is dissolved. Simmer syrup 5 minutes and cool. Stir in juices.

Divide drink among 6 tall glasses filled with ice cubes and garnish with mint sprigs. Makes about 6 cups, serving 6.

Rich Hot Chocolate

6 cups milk
9 ounces fine-quality bittersweet chocolate, chopped fine
2 teaspoons vanilla
1/2 cup well-chilled heavy cream

Garnish: fine-quality bittersweet chocolate shavings

In a large heavy saucepan combine milk and a pinch of salt and bring just to a boil over moderate heat. In a small heatproof bowl combine chocolate with about 1 cup hot milk mixture and whisk until chocolate is melted and mixture is smooth. Whisk chocolate mixture into remaining milk mixture and simmer, whisking, 2 minutes. Remove hot chocolate from heat and stir in vanilla. (For a frothy drink, in a blender blend hot chocolate in batches.) In a small bowl beat cream until it holds soft peaks.

Divide hot chocolate among 6 mugs and top with whipped cream. Garnish drinks with chocolate shavings. Makes about 7 cups, serving 6.

Index

C

Table Setting Acknowledgments

ANY ITEMS IN THE
PHOTOGRAPHS NOT
CREDITED ARE
PRIVATELY OWNED.
ALL ADDRESSES ARE
IN NEW YORK CITY
UNLESS OTHERWISE
INDICATED.

JACKET

**CHILLED TOMATO BASIL SOUP;
GARLIC BAGUETTE TOASTS**
Mottahedeh "Torquay" ironstone
plates—The Winterthur Museum
Store on Clenny Run, tel. (800)
448-3883. Schott-Zwiesel "Crystal
Boutique" bowls—Cardel, Ltd., 621
Madison Avenue. "Chinon" silver-
plate flatware—Pavillon Christofle,
680 Madison Avenue.

SPRING GARDEN WEEKEND
MUSSEL AND PARSLEY SOUP
(page 12): Hand-thrown stoneware
soup bowls by Richard Batterham—
Simon Pearce, 385 Bleeker Street.
"Tema" stoneware dinner plates by
Bing & Grondahl—Royal
Copenhagen Porcelain/Georg Jensen
Silversmiths, 683 Madison Avenue.
"Silver Shell" silver-plate flatware—
Oneida Silversmiths, Oneida, New
York. Nineteenth-century cherry farm
table—Howard Kaplan Antiques,
827 Broadway.
**COFFEE COFFEECAKE WITH
ESPRESSO GLAZE** (page 16):
"Borderie Normande" cotton fabric
(available through decorator)—
Brunschwig & Fils, Inc., 979 Third
Avenue.
**MIXED LETTUCES WITH CITRUS
DRESSING** (page 20): French
faience luncheon plates—Solanée,
866 Lexington Avenue. Hand-forged
"Feather Edge" sterling flatware—
James Robinson, 480 Park Avenue.
"Brummel" crystal water goblets and
wineglasses; "Swirl" saltcellar and pep-
per cellar and ivory spoons—
Baccarat, Inc., 625 Madison Avenue.
"Grapevine" cotton fabric (available
through decorator)—Cowtan & Tout,
979 Third Avenue.

**GOAT CHEESE RAVIOLI WITH
GARLIC TOMATO SAUCE** (page 24):
"White Fan" porcelain dinner plate—
Royal Copenhagen Porcelain/Georg
Jensen Silversmiths, 683 Madison
Avenue.
**CAPPUCCINO GELATO;
CHOCOLATE NUT COOKIES**
(page 30): Glass dessert bowls—
Barneys New York, Seventh Avenue
and Seventeenth Street. Twig table—
Zona, 97 Greene Street.

**SUMMER BEACH HOUSE
WEEKEND**
RASPBERRY CORN MUFFINS
(page 40): "Bennet's Bridge" hand-
decorated earthenware dinner plates,
dessert plates, and coffee mugs
designed by Sybil Connolly—Tiffany,
727 Fifth Avenue. English bone and
silver flatware, circa 1800 (from a set
of 6 knives and forks)—Gail Lettick's
Pantry & Hearth, 121 East 35th
Street. Glass pitcher and tumblers;
silver-plate coffeepot, sugar, and
creamer, circa 1900 (one of a
kind)—Wolfman • Gold & Good
Company, 116 Greene Street. Cotton
tablecloth and napkins by Paula
Sweet—Bergdorf Goodman, 754 Fifth
Avenue.
**MARINATED BLACK AND GREEN
OLIVES; CRUDITÉS WITH
RAVIGOTE MAYONNAISE;
PROVENÇALE SANDWICHES WITH
TUNA, BASIL, AND TOMATO**
(page 44): Lead basket; cotton fabrics
—Pierre Deux, 870 Madison Avenue.
Shell, ceramic crocks, Wüsthof white-
handled sandwich knife, corkscrew,
and pepper mill—Bridge
Kitchenware Corporation, 214 East
52nd Street. Large wicker basket with
tray insert—Wolfman • Gold & Good

Company, 116 Greene Street. French rilsan and rattan chaise with detachable foot rest—T & K French Antiques, Inc., 120 Wooster Street. "Wildflower" cotton-terry cloth towels—D. Porthault, 18 East 69th Street. Fieldcrest white cotton-terry cloth towels—Bloomingdales, 1000 Third Avenue.

FROZEN NECTARINE MOUSSE WITH BLACKBERRY SWIRL (page 52): Earthenware dessert plates by Barbara Eigen—Afton Grove, 1000 Torrey Pines Road, La Jolla, CA. Silver-plate cake server—Wolfman • Gold & Good Company, 116 Greene Street.

FALL FOLIAGE WEEKEND
SPICY MACARONI AND CHEESE (page 62): Porcelain baking dish in straw server—Wolfman • Gold & Good Company, 116 Greene Street. **OATMEAL CINNAMON TUILES; APPLE AND CARAMEL SORBETS** (page 66): Ceramic bowls, wood "leaf" plates, plaid wool blanket (from a collection)—AdHoc Softwares 410 West Broadway. **STEAK WITH PEPPERCORNS; FRIED SHOESTRING POTATOES; HERBED TOMATOES** (page 70): Silver-plate and enamel candlesticks—Puiforcat, 811 Madison Avenue. French cherry wood table, circa 1860—Pierre Deux Antiques, 369 Bleeker Street.

WHITE BEAN AND VEGETABLE SOUP (page 76): Italian ceramic soup bowl and dinner plate by Grazia-Deruta; "Pointus" stainless-steel soup spoon by Phillipe Starck—The L • S Collection, 765 Madison Avenue. French porcelain tureen by Apilco—Williams-Sonoma, 20 East 60th Street. Cotton napkin—Dean & DeLuca Inc., 560 Broadway.

WINTER SKI WEEKEND
CHICKEN AND GARBANZO STEW (page 82): Nineteenth-century English ceramic soup plate; nineteenth-century pewter spoon and wooden-handled flatware; hand-woven cotton napkins; nineteenth-century Dutch painted bread board—Gail Lettick's Pantry & Hearth Antiques, 121 East 35th Street. **MULTIGRAIN GRANOLA** (page 86): Twig console—Pottery Barn, 117 East 59th Street. **MEXICAN BEAN SOUP** (page 90): "Black Jasmine" soup plate and bowls—Zona, 97 Greene Street. **PRUNE ARMAGNAC GINGERBREAD** (page 94): "Empire" bone china plates—Polo Ralph Lauren, 867 Madison Avenue. Cotton napkins by Paula Sweet—Frank McIntosh Shop at Henri Bendel, 712 Fifth Avenue. Flowers—Zezé 398 East 52nd Street. **FUSILLI WITH COLLARDS, BACON, AND GARLIC** (page 98): "Green Leaf" ceramic soup bowls and dinner plates; cotton place mats and napkins; "Oak Leaf" painted metal napkin rings—Pottery Barn, 117 East 59th Street.

MORE BREAKFAST AND BRUNCH DISHES
CORNMEAL PORRIDGE WITH DRIED FRUIT (page 102): English "King's Rose" creamware bowl, plate, cream pitcher, and sugar bowl; cotton napkin; nineteenth-century cotton tablecloth; nineteenth-century tole syrup cup; and tin tray—Gail Lettick's Pantry & Hearth Antiques, 121 East 35th Street. **TARRAGON SCRAMBLED EGGS IN TULIP CROUSTADES** (page 113): Hand-woven cotton and linen napkin—Frank McIntosh Shop at Henri Bendel, 712 Fifth Avenue.

MORE LUNCH ENTRÉES
BUTTERNUT SQUASH SOUP WITH GINGER AND LIME; ASIAGO TOASTS (page 118): Christofle Capricorne Collection "Touraine" stainless-steel flatware—Pavillon Christofle, 680 Madison Avenue. "Tulip" hand-blown wineglasses—Simon Pearce, 500 Park Avenue. Linen napkins—Frank McIntosh Shop at Henri Bendel, 712 Fifth Avenue. English Doulton stoneware open salts, circa 1878—James II Galleries, Ltd., 11 East 57th Street. Polished iron and brass table base—Howard Kaplan Antiques, 827 Broadway.

WHEAT BERRY AND BARLEY SALAD WITH SMOKED MOZZARELLA (page 126): China salad plates and dinner plates; acrylic wineglasses; bamboo place mats by Chateau X—Frank McIntosh Shop at Henri Bendel, 712 Fifth Avenue. Sasaki "Wallis" stainless-steel flatware—Adrien Linford, 1320 Madison Avenue.
BARBECUE PORK BURGER WITH COLESLAW; THAI-STYLE TURKEY BURGER WITH PICKLED CUCUMBERS; AND GREEK-STYLE LAMB BURGER WITH MINTED YOGURT SAUCE (page 130): English hand-polished aluminum plates—MoMA Design Store, 44 West 53rd Street.

MORE DINNER ENTRÉES
RED PORK AND BEAN CHILI; TURKEY CHIPOTLE CHILI; NEW MEXICAN PORK AND GREEN CHILI STEW; AND BLACK BEAN AND ANCHO CHILI (page 153): Mexican handmade ceramic bowls; handwoven cotton place mats—Pan American Phoenix, The Market at Citicorp Center, 153 East 53rd Street.
VEAL STEW (page 157): Pinchon faience platter; pewter vegetable dish; Sèvres pewter and crystal wineglasses; pewter candlestick; cotton tablecloth —Pierre Deux, 870 Madison Avenue.

MORE SIDE DISHES
MIXED GREENS WITH GRAPEFRUIT, FENNEL, AND PARMESAN (page 158): Stainless-steel servers— The Pottery Barn, 117 East 59th Street. Wedgwood "Nantucket Basket" bone china bowls—Waterford Wedgwood, 713 Madison Avenue.

GREEN BEAN, RED ONION, AND ROASTED POTATO SALAD WITH ROSEMARY VINAIGRETTE; COUSCOUS TABBOULEH; ANTIPASTO PASTA SALAD; AND CURRIED RICE SALAD WITH MELON, RAISINS, AND PEANUTS (page 167): Star-shaped ceramic plates—Wolfman • Gold & Good Co., 116 Greene Street.
CORN BREAD, SAUSAGE, AND SCALLION STUFFING; RAISIN BREAD, CRANBERRY, AND ROSEMARY STUFFING; GREEN CHILI STUFFING; AND MASHED POTATO AND SAUTÉED APPLE STUFFING (page 173): Handmade ceramic bowls—Eigen Arts, 150 Bay Street, Jersey City, NJ 07302, tel. (201) 798-7310. Eighteenth- and nineteenth-century sterling stuffing spoons—S. Wyler, 941 Lexington Avenue; J. Mavec & Company Ltd., 625 Madison Avenue.

MORE DESSERTS
BLUEBERRY BUTTERMILK TART AND BLUEBERRY ICE CREAM (page 174): Green ceramic plate by Molin—Barneys New York, Seventh Avenue and 17th Street.
CARROT RAISIN CAKE WITH IRISH CREAM FROSTING (page 179): Wedgwood drabware dessert plates, circa 1820 (from a set of 10)— Bardith Ltd., 901 Madison Avenue.

OHIO SHAKER LEMON PIE; CRANBERRY RAISIN TART (page 183): Dried herbs and flowers—Shale Hill Farm & Herb Gardens, 6856 Hommelville Road, Saugerties, NY 12477.
COCONUT PARFAITS; ROSÉ SORBET (page 190): "Rosalino Rigadin" parfait glasses designed by Carlo Moretti— Avventura, 463 Amsterdam Avenue.

MORE SNACKS AND BEVERAGES
YELLOW BELL PEPPER SALSA WITH CUMIN TORTILLA CHIPS; CHILI ALMONDS AND COCONUT CHIPS (page 192): "Tuscany" wineglasses—Wolfman • Gold & Good Company, 116 Greene Street. Earthenware bowls by Barbara Eigen; hand-woven runner by Muffy Young—Zona, 97 Greene Street. Hand-painted wooden tray (holding vegetables, as centerpiece)—Portico, 379 West Broadway. Cedar table, circa 1850, and handmade ironwood chairs—Statement on Montana, 1302 Montana Avenue, Santa Monica, CA.
PIMM'S CUPS AND CHEDDAR TWISTS (page 197): "Ingmar" glasses designed by Henning Koppel for Orrefors—Orrefors Kosta Boda Galleri, 58 East 57th Street. English silver-plate basket with green opaline glass liner, circa 1870; Art Deco porcelain and metal tray—James II Galleries, Ltd., 11 East 57th Street.
MANGO WINE COOLER; BLUE LAGOON; PLANTER'S PUNCH; AND MELON BALL (page 202): "Pavillon" crystal goblets—Baccarat, Inc., 625 Madison Avenue.

THE FOLLOWING PHOTOGRAPHERS
HAVE GENEROUSLY GIVEN THEIR PERMISSION
TO REPRINT THE PHOTOGRAPHS LISTED OPPOSITE.
MANY HAVE PREVIOUSLY APPEARED IN
GOURMET MAGAZINE.

LANS CHRISTENSEN: "Hale Farm and Village, OH" (page 2); Tulips at Monticello, VA (page 10); "Azaleas at The Boar's Head Inn, VA" (page 19); "Morven Gardens, VA" (page 29); "Part of Ohio's Apple Harvest" (page 60); "Hang Gliding in Telluride, CO" (page 89). Copyright © 1987. "Weston Village Store, VT" (page 6); "Baldy's Reflection and Summit, Sun Valley, ID" (page 93). Copyright © 1990.
LISA KOENIG: "Hydrangeas on a Trellis" (page 51). Copyright © 1994.
ANGELO LOMEO: "Foliage Down a Winding Road in Shelburne, MA" (pages 74 and 75). Copyright © 1990.
MATHIAS OPPERSDORFF: "Great Salt Pond on Block Island, RI" (page 54). Copyright © 1989.
ADAM WOOLFITT: "High above Saint-Moritz, Switzerland" (page 101). Copyright © 1994.
ROMULO A. YANES: "Corn in Black Basket" (page 34). Copyright © 1985. "Birds on Cayo Costa, FL" (page 43). Copyright © 1989.

GRATEFUL ACKNOWLEDGMENT IS MADE
TO THE FOLLOWING CONTRIBUTORS FOR
PERMISSION TO REPRINT RECIPES PREVIOUSLY
PUBLISHED IN *GOURMET* MAGAZINE.

NAOMI BARRY AND BETTINA MCNULTY: "Chocolate Crème Brûlées" (page 74). Copyright © 1991.
JAYNE COHEN: "Goat Cheese Ravioli with Garlic Tomato Sauce" (page 26). Copyright © 1990.
GEORGIA CHAN DOWNARD: "Marinated Seafood and Blood Orange Salad" (page 147). Copyright © 1988.
JOHN GOLDEN: "Butter-Rich Fudge Brownies" (page 47). Copyright © 1991.
SUSAN HERRMANN LOOMIS: "Chicken and Garbanzo Stew" (page 84). Copyright © 1991.
DEBORAH MADISON: "Spaghetti with Handfuls of Herbs" (page 58). Copyright © 1990.
DORIAN LEIGH PARKER: "Veal Stew" (page 156). Copyright © 1990.
RICHARD SAX: "Prune and Pecan Caramel Sticky Buns" (page 106). Copyright © 1988. "Coffee Coffeecake with Espresso Glaze"(page 18). Copyright © 1989.
SALLY TAGER: "Mexican Bean Soup" (page 92). Copyright © 1990.